Marie M. Fortune
Joretta L. Marshall
Editors

Forgiveness and Abuse: Jewish and Christian Reflections

Forgiveness and Abuse: Jewish and Christian Reflections has been co-published as *Journal of Religion & Abuse*, Volume 4, Number 4 2002.

Pre-Publication
REVIEWS,
COMMENTARIES,
EVALUATIONS . . .

"**P**ROFOUNDLY SIGNIFICANT. . . . Uncovering both the misconceptions and the possibilities of forgiveness in the context of radical brokenness, this work makes possible the partnership of justice and transformative healing."

Kristen J. Leslie, PhD,
Assistant Professor of Pastoral Care and Counseling
Yale University Divinity School

"**A**s a Catholic priest/psycho-therapist who has jour-neyed with survivors of sexual abuse for more than twenty years, I found this to be AN EXTREMELY HELPFUL COLLECTION of essays. If our churches and synagogues are serious about becoming mor responsive to the crisis of abuse, this book will be A VALUED RESOURCE. The book confronts the tendency toward over-sprituial-izing by approaching forgiveness as a complex and nuanced pro-cess."

Rev. John Heagle, MA, JCL
Co-Director of Therapy &
Renewal Associates
Adjunct Faculty Member
in the School of Theology &
Ministry at Seattle University
Co-Author of Tender Fires:
The Spiritual Promise of Sexuality

The Haworth Pastoral Press
An Imprint of The Haworth Press, Inc.

Forgiveness and Abuse:
Jewish and Christian Reflections

Forgiveness and Abuse: Jewish and Christian Reflections has been co-published simultaneously as *Journal of Religion & Abuse*, Volume 4, Number 4 2002.

The *Journal of Religion & Abuse* Monographic "Separates"

Below is a list of "separates," which in serials librarianship means a special issue simultaneously published as a special journal issue or double-issue *and* as a "separate" hardbound monograph. (This is a format which we also call a "DocuSerial.")

"Separates" are published because specialized libraries or professionals may wish to purchase a specific thematic issue by itself in a format which can be separately cataloged and shelved, as opposed to purchasing the journal on an on-going basis. Faculty members may also more easily consider a "separate" for classroom adoption.

"Separates" are carefully classified separately with the major book jobbers so that the journal tie-in can be noted on new book order slips to avoid duplicate purchasing.

You may wish to visit Haworth's Website at . . .

http://www.HaworthPress.com

. . . to search our online catalog for complete tables of contents of these separates and related publications.

You may also call 1-800-HAWORTH (outside US/Canada: 607-722-5857), or Fax 1-800-895-0582 (outside US/Canada: 607-771-0012), or e-mail at:

docdelivery@haworthpress.com

Forgiveness and Abuse: Jewish and Christian Reflections, edited by Marie M. Fortune, MDiv, DHLit, and Joretta L. Marshall, PhD, MDiv, (Vol. 4, No. 4, 2002). *"PROFOUNDLY SIGNIFICANT. . . . Uncovering both the misconceptions and the possibilities of forgiveness in the context of radical brokenness, this work makes possible the partnership of justice and transformative healing . . ." Kristen J. Leslie, PhD, Assistant Professor of Pastoral Care and Counseling, Yale University Divinity School)*

Remembering Conquest: Feminist/Womanist Perspectives on Religion, Colonization, and Sexual Violence, edited by Nantawan Boonprasat Lewis, BDiv, ThM, PhD, and Marie M. Fortune, MDiv, DHLit (Vol. 1, No. 2, 1999). *Addresses the issue of sexual violence against Native American, African American, Filipino, and Thai women from feminist/womanist theological perspectives and advocates for change in how some religious groups interpret women.*

Forgiveness and Abuse: Jewish and Christian Reflections

Marie M. Fortune, MDiv, DHLit
Joretta L. Marshall, PhD, MDiv
Editors

Forgiveness and Abuse: Jewish and Christian Reflections has been co-published simultaneously as *Journal of Religion & Abuse*, Volume 4, Number 4 2002.

The Haworth Pastoral Press®
An Imprint of The Haworth Press, Inc.

New York • London • Victoria (AU)
www.HaworthPress.com

Forgiveness and Abuse: Jewish and Christian Reflections has been co-published simultaneously as *Journal of Religion & Abuse*, Volume 4, Number 4 2002.

Cover design by Brooke Stiles.

Library of Congress Cataloging-in-Publication Data

Forgiveness and abuse: Jewish and Christian reflections / Marie M. Fortune, Joretta L. Marshall, editors.

    p. cm.
    "Co-published simultaneously as Journal of religion & abuse, volume 4, number 4 2002."
    Includes bibliographical references and index.
    ISBN 0-7890-2251-6 (hc) – ISBN 0-7890-2252-4 (pbk.)
    1. Forgiveness–Religious aspects–Judaism. 2. Forgiveness–Religious aspects–Christianity. 3. Offenses against the person. 4. Forgiveness–Psycholgoical aspects. Child sexual abuse by clergy. 6. Foregiveness–Fiction. I. Fortune, Marie M. II. Marshall, Joretta L. III Journal of religion & abuse.
BJ1286.F67F67 2003
261.8'327–dc22   2003018153

Indexing, Abstracting & Website/Internet Coverage

This section provides you with a list of major indexing & abstracting services. That is to say, each service began covering this periodical during the year noted in the right column. Most Websites which are listed below have indicated that they will either post, disseminate, compile, archive, cite or alert their own Website users with research-based content from this work. (This list is as current as the copyright date of this publication.)

Abstracting, Website/Indexing Coverage . . . . Year When Coverage Began

- *Ageline Database* **2000**
- *CNPIEC Reference Guide: Chinese National Directory
  of Foreign Periodicals* **1999**
- *Contemporary Women's Issues* **1999**
- *Criminal Justice Abstracts* **1999**
- *e-psyche, LLC <http://www.e-psyche.net>* **2001**
- *Family & Society Studies Worldwide
  <http://www.nisc.com>* **1999**
- *Family Index Database <http://www.familyscholar.com>* **2003**
- *Family Violence & Sexual Assault Bulletin* **1999**
- *FRANCIS INIST/CNRS <http://www.inist.fr>* **1999**
- *Guide to Social Science & Religion in Periodical Literature* **1999**
- *IBZ International Bibliography of Periodical Literature
  <http://www.saur.de>* **1999**
- *Index to Jewish Periodicals <http://www.jewishperiodicals.com>* . . . **2001**
- *Index to Periodical Articles Related to Law* **1999**
- *Linguistics and Language Behavior Abstracts (LLBA)
  <http://www.csa.com>* **2000**

(continued)

Special Bibliographic Notes related to special journal issues (separates) and indexing/abstracting:

- indexing/abstracting services in this list will also cover material in any "separate" that is co-published simultaneously with Haworth's special thematic journal issue or DocuSerial. Indexing/abstracting usually covers material at the article/chapter level.
- monographic co-editions are intended for either non-subscribers or libraries which intend to purchase a second copy for their circulating collections.
- monographic co-editions are reported to all jobbers/wholesalers/approval plans. The source journal is listed as the "series" to assist the prevention of duplicate purchasing in the same manner utilized for books-in-series.
- to facilitate user/access services all indexing/abstracting services are encouraged to utilize the co-indexing entry note indicated at the bottom of the first page of each article/chapter/contribution.
- this is intended to assist a library user of any reference tool (whether print, electronic, online, or CD-ROM) to locate the monographic version if the library has purchased this version but not a subscription to the source journal.

Forgiveness and Abuse:
Jewish and Christian Reflections

CONTENTS

ABOUT THE EDITORS

Marie M. Fortune, MDiv, DHLit, is Founder and Senior Analyst of the Center for the Prevention of Sexual and Domestic Violence in Seattle, Washington, an educational ministry serving as a training resource to religious communities in the United States and Canada. A pastor, educator, and practicing ethicist and theologian, she is the author of several books, including *Is Nothing Sacred? When Sex Invades the Pastoral Relationship*, which won the 1990 Book of the Year Award from the Academy of Parish Clergy. Rev. Fortune received her seminary training at Yale Divinity School and was ordained a minister in the United Church of Christ in 1976. She has been recognized for her dedicated work, most recently receiving the International Peace Award from the Reorganized Church of Jesus Christ of Latter Day Saints in 1998.

Joretta L. Marshall, PhD, MDiv, is Academic Dean and Professor of Pastoral Theology and Care at Eden Theological Seminary in St. Louis, Missouri. She received her Master of Divinity from Iliff School of Theology in Denver, Colorado and a Master of Arts and PhD from Vanderbilt University in Nashville, Tennessee.

Prior to joining the faculty at Eden, Joretta served on the faculties of Vanderbilt University Divinity School (1989-1993) and Iliff School of Theology (1993-2001).

During her career she has also served as a college chaplain, an Assistant and Associate pastor of two local churches, and a pastoral counselor. Joretta is an ordained Elder in the United Methodist Church, Rocky Mountain Conference.

Throughout her academic career Dr. Marshall has retained membership in the American Association of Pastoral Counselors (AAPC). She has been a regional chair for the Rocky Mountain/Plains Region and is currently part of a national AAPC task force on formation. As a pastoral counselor she has worked with agencies, churches, individuals and families in seeking healing and wholeness.

Dr. Marshall's current publishing interests include her work as the Co-Editor for the *Journal of Pastoral Theology*, a publication supported by the Society for Pastoral Theology. She is writing in the area of forgiveness, justice and community, and hopes to have a manuscript completed in the coming year. She is the author of *Counseling Lesbian Partners*, along with a number of articles in professional and church-related journals. Her work in pastoral care and counseling focuses on issues of gender, sexuality, developmental theory, pedagogy in theological education, and prophetic pastoral care.

About the Contributors

Margaret Arms is Executive Director of The Shalom Center in Colorado Springs, CO, USA, an interfaith resource addressing spiritual issues of people affected by trauma. She is also an adjunct faculty member at the Colorado School of Professional Psychology where she teaches religion and psychology. In addition to being a licensed clinical social worker, she holds a PhD in religious and theological studies in the area of religion and psychology from the University of Denver and Iliff School of Theology.

Marilyn Born was a founding member of the first support and advocacy group in Australia (SHIVERS, Sexual Harassment Is Violence, Effective Redress Stops it) for adult women making complaints of harassment, abuse and assault to churches and secular agencies. SHIVERS was the first to publicly name clergy violence as well as role playing and documenting Christian [sic] church leaders responses to formal complaints at a National Conference of Women in Melbourne, Australia, in 1990. Marilyn has written on Domestic Violence and Clergy Violence in faith communities for parishioners and Violence Against Women in general for a Deakin University text. She has a B.Litt from Deakin University (Women's Studies) and a BA from Harvard Extension.

Catherine Coyle is a registered nurse and holds a master's degree in psychiatric nursing as well as a doctoral degree in educational psychology, both from the University of Wisconsin in Madison. She is an associate of the International Forgiveness Institute and has held teaching positions at UW-Madison and Edgewood College.

Mark Dratch is the Senior Rabbi of Congregation Agudath Sholom, Stamford, CT, USA, a member of the Jewish Advisory Committee of the Center for the Prevention of Sexual and Domestic Violence, and a member of the Editorial Board of the *Journal of Religion & Abuse*. He is treasurer of the Rabbinical Council of America and an instructor on Judaic Studies at the Isaac Breuer College of Yeshiva University, New

York. He received his rabbinic ordination at the Rabbi Isaac Elchanan Theological Seminary of Yeshiva University.

James S. Evinger is a clinical researcher at the University of Rochester Medical Center, and is a chaplain for New York State Office of Mental Retardation/Developmental Disabilities, Rochester, NY, USA. He is an ordained minister, Presbyterian Church (USA).

Todd A. Heim received his master's degree in clinical psychology at the University of Dayton and currently works as a therapist at the Family & Children's Center in Indiana, USA.

Dr. Peter Horsfield is Senior Lecturer in Communication and Manager of Development Projects for the School of Applied Communication at RMIT University in Melbourne, Australia. He was Dean of the Uniting Church Theological Hall and Lecturer in Practical Theology at the United Faculty of Theology in Melbourne from 1987-1996. His position was terminated through redefinition following his advocacy work in the area of clergy professional misconduct.

Jane McAvoy is Interim Academic Dean and Visiting Associate Professor of Theology at St. Paul School of Theology in Kansas City, Missouri. She has an MDiv from Lexington Theological Seminary and a PhD in theology from the University of Chicago. She is an ordained minister of the Christian Church (Disciples of Christ).

Nancy Poling is the writing tutor at Kendall College in Evanston, Illinois, USA, and a freelance writer/editor. She is the editor of *From Victim To Survivor: Women Recovering From Clergy Sexual Abuse* (United Church Press, 1999). "When Sisters Dream" is from her unpublished collection: *Matriarch And Giant Slayer: Might-Have-Been Women From Hebrew Scripture.*

Mark S. Rye is currently Assistant Professor in the psychology department at the University of Dayton in Ohio, USA.

Marcia Cohn Spiegel, Jewish Communal Service, Hebrew Union College/Jewish Institute of Religion, is a community activist and is working to create change in the attitudes of the Jewish community towards addiction, violence and sexual abuse. She is the founder of the Alcohol/Drug Workshop of Jewish Family Service, Los Angeles, and *L'Chaim*: A 12-step program for recovery. She sits on the Jewish Advisory Committee of the Center for Prevention of Sexual and Domestic Violence and is the author of *The Heritage of Noah: Alcoholism in the Jewish Community Today*, and co-author of *The Jewish Women's Awareness Guide,* and *Women Speak to God: The Poems and Prayers of Jewish Women.*

Dorthea L. Yoder is pastor, Summerville Presbyterian Church, Irondequoit, NY, USA. She is an ordained minister, Presbyterian Church (USA), and has chaired the Committee on Ministry, Presbytery of Genesee Valley, NY.

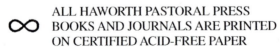

Introduction

Marie M. Fortune
Joretta L. Marshall

At the heart of the healing process for many victims and survivors of abuse rests the question of forgiveness. Who needs to be forgiven for what? Is it time to forgive? Can I forgive someone who never says "I'm sorry"? How does withholding forgiveness from someone slow down or impede my own healing process? Are there some atrocities too deep and evil for the term "forgiveness" to hold meaning? These same questions are asked, not only by the individuals who experience abuse, but also by persons and groups who have experienced any kind of injustice or wrong. In the face of hurt, injustice, and wrong-doing, what is the role and place of forgiveness?

When thinking about responses to feelings of hurt and pain it is not unusual for those who have been wronged or harmed to turn to their religious traditions for assistance, insight, and direction. Every major religious tradition has some way of responding to the wrongs or injustices done to individuals or communities.

In Judaism, forgiveness is part of the process of *teshuvah*, repentance and return to a state of wholeness. This process is central to the fall High Holy Day season and especially Yom Kippur, the Day of Atonement, which encourages taking responsibility for the harm one may have caused to others. Acknowledging that responsibility is the first step towards rectifying the harm and seeking forgiveness.

[Haworth co-indexing entry note]: "Introduction." Fortune, Marie M., and Joretta L. Marshall. Co-published simultaneously in Journal of Religion & Abuse (The Haworth Pastoral Practice Press, an imprint of The Haworth Press, Inc.) Vol. 4, No. 4, 2002, pp. 1-5; and: *Forgiveness and Abuse: Jewish and Christian Reflections* (ed: Marie M. Fortune, and Joretta L. Marshall) The Haworth Pastoral Practice Press, an imprint of The Haworth Press, Inc., 2002, pp. 1-5. Single or multiple copies of this article are available for a fee from The Haworth Document Delivery Service [1-800-HAWORTH, 9:00 a.m. - 5:00 p.m. (EST). E-mail address: docdelivery@haworthpress.com].

Journal of Religion and Abuse, Vol 4(4) 2002
http://www.haworthpress.com/store/product.asp?sku=J154
10.1300J154v04n04_01

In the Christian tradition, the burden of action has often been placed on the victim regardless of the actions of the perpetrator. Nonetheless, forgiveness has been one of the vehicles for grace as persons and/or families struggle with the wrongs they have experienced at the hands of others. At times, the notion of forgiveness can become freeing and liberating as individuals discover the gift that comes with not only finding ways to forgive those who have wronged them, but with being able to be forgiven for the transgressions one makes in relationship.

At the same time, while religious traditions assist people in thinking about how best to respond to the wrongs that have been done to them, one's faith tradition can also become a place of experiencing further abuse or shame. Forgiveness sometimes becomes another way of hurting and wronging others. In other words, the demand to forgive so that everyone will feel better, or the desire to minimize conflict in relationships, encourages "forgiveness" that is too quick and, ultimately, not redemptive. In this sense, forgiveness becomes part of the problem rather than part of the healing process.

There are several significant facts about forgiveness that many of the authors in this collection articulate. First, at the very least, there is a mutual recognition that forgiveness has something to do with one's system of belief or religious tradition. The content and movement of the forgiveness process is, in large part, dependent upon one's religious belief system. For some, the process becomes a way of re-discovering and re-inventing relationships that are grounded in such things as justice, love, and mutuality. For others, it is a process that brings one to a deepened understanding and experience of God's redemptive love. For still others, forgiveness is a process of being in right relationships with God, self, and others. In the articles that follow you will find different understandings of the religious content of forgiveness, its purpose and its direction. What is present in all of them, however, is the notion that forgiveness has something to do with one's religious beliefs and is somehow connected with the possibility of healing.

Second, most of the authors in this series of articles note that forgiveness takes time. It is not something that happens quickly; indeed it is not something that should happen so soon and so painlessly that the depth and hurt of the wrong is quickly dismissed. In other words, forgiveness cannot be perfunctory or superficial; it must be genuine and real. There is a strong sense that the deeper the hurt or wound to the individual, family, or community, the longer and slower the process will be. If the wrong was committed during one's childhood, as in child sexual or physical abuse, one can suspect that the damage done to one's inner core is incredibly deep. Additionally, if the hurt occurred over a long period of time, such as repeated abuse, then the forgiveness process becomes prolonged and deep. One of the reasons why encouraging forgiveness too quickly, or demanding forgiveness when one is not yet ready is counterproductive is that if we are to take seriously forgiveness as a process that works on inner healing, we must allow for such healing to take the time and energy it needs to do the work. Moving too quickly in this process brings good to no one, including the offender and the victim.

Third, it is clear that forgiveness is a relational process. This does not mean that one must be engaged in person with the one who has done the harm; rather to suggest that forgiveness is a relational process recognizes only that forgiveness is difficult and painful work because the hurt occurs in the context of relationship. At times, it is possible that the forgiveness process occurs with the person who has done the wrong, but it is clear that this is not always the case. In fact, in some situations, it is dangerous and harmful to insist that the person who has done the wrong participate intimately in the process. Only when there is mutual regard, safety, and genuine care between persons can forgiveness happen within the context of the relationship itself. What is clear, however, is that the process never occurs outside of some kind of relationship with one's higher power, with friends, with family, with pastoral caregivers and counselors, and with one's community.

Finally, one needs to ask about the goal or purpose of forgiveness. Is forgiveness for the one who has offended, or is it part of the healing process for the one who has been hurt? Perhaps one of the mysteries and gifts of forgiveness for those who have experienced it comes with the recognition that forgiveness frees both participants in ways that are quite remarkable.

Perhaps the question before one who has been abused or victimized is not "should I forgive?" but rather "can I forgive?" The question for all of us in community is what can we do to help free those who have been harmed to forgive? How do we assist people to let go and move forward with their own healing process? Too often well-meaning friends, family and faith communities have urged individuals to "forgive and forget" (Shakespeare's *King Lear*) as a panacea which frees the rest of us from sharing the burden of harm that the individual bears. It never works and only serves to isolate the victim even further.

Rather, we should be seeking ways to forgive and remember. This means that we in community help create the conditions that make forgiveness possible. These conditions can best be described as justice-making. When people have experienced trauma and abuse, they need to be able to recount their experience and have it heard and understood by the people around them. In responding, we as community need to hear and acknowledge and provide a moral framework that says that what was done to them was wrong and should never have happened. Then we must be willing to walk with them in the aftermath; do everything we can to protect others from further harm; and call the person who harmed them to account; and try to find ways that the abuser or community can make restitution to the survivor. All of this finally can result in vindication for the survivor. To be vindicated is to be set free, even bearing scars, to get on with one's life. There is seldom perfect justice but often approximate justice is sufficient. How can we help make justice happen for each other?

The other aspect of forgiveness that we often overlook is the impact of superficial, premature forgiveness on perpetrators and those who have caused harm to another. To announce that someone is "forgiven" even before they have acknowledged the harm they have done, denies them the opportunity for repentance and change. The prophet Ezekiel says that to repent is to get a new mind and new heart which means to be accountable and to strive never to repeat the harmful behavior again. Quick forgiveness short-circuits the process; it serves no one's interests except the wider community in supposedly relieving us of our collective responsibility to help make justice.

If there is one area to deepen in our studies of forgiveness, it is in response to concerns about the complexity and depth of forgiveness when it involves more than two or three people. For example, in cases where a community is wronged or harmed, how does the community begin to move toward forgiveness? Work such as that being done by the Truth and Reconciliation Committee in South Africa, or the Project to Recover the Historical Memory in Guatemala provide insight and clues to the power and process of forgiveness at broader, communal levels.

In this volume, you will find many authors who bring their faith perspectives, their religious understandings, and their skills as theologians, scientists, writers, and theorists to the conversation of forgiveness. The traditions of Judaism and Christianity are represented here and the interplay theologically and ethically between these two traditions is much in evidence in these articles. The next phase of this discussion should include other traditions so that we might learn from the insights of each.

Rabbi Mark Dratch provides insight into the connection between repentance and forgiveness by examining the Written and Oral Law of the Jewish tradition. His assessment of the various resources brings him to the conclusion that repentance and justice are central to meaningful forgiveness. His reading of the Jewish tradition leads him to conclude that without contrition and change of behavior, forgiveness is not attainable.

Marcia Cohn Spiegel provides a commentary on forgiveness and the High Holy Days which is an important application of Jewish teaching to real life and important communal rituals. In tandem with the commentary is a prayer developed by the Shalom Bayit Program at Jewish Family and Career Services in Atlanta, Georgia, USA. The prayer is used on Yom Kippur and speaks to those who have experienced abuse in their homes and families.

Todd A. Heim and Mark S. Rye compare and contrast Jewish and Christian approaches to forgiveness in the context of mental health. This is a study of congregants from Midwest U.S. churches and synagogues. The results were somewhat surprising.

Peter Horsfield critiques the loss of an ethical framework in Christian churches' use and misuse of forgiveness. He situates his discussion within his work on the problem of clergy misconduct in Australian churches. Utilizing the traditional Samoan practice of *Ifonga,* he explores the possibilities of placing forgiveness within an ethical context.

James S. Evinger and Dorthea L. Yoder follow with vignettes and commentary again focused on clergy misconduct in U.S. Protestant congregations. They present a substantive look at the problems and possibilities of forgiveness and the importance of justice in the concrete situations of judicatory response to clergy misconduct.

Catherine T. Coyle examines forgiveness and reconciliation in the context of abuse. She questions the tendency to equate the two and suggests a process model of forgiveness that emphasizes psychological healing.

Margaret F. Arms draws upon her clinical experience as a therapist and her work on theodicy and evil to conclude that truth-telling is one of the vital aspects in forgiveness. In particular, she looks at the public and private aspects of forgiveness, noting the significance that truth has in moving individuals and communities toward forgiveness. Building on earlier work done by Marie Fortune, Arms advances the conversation on truth-telling by developing a deeper connection with notions of complicity and resistance.

Jane McAvoy draws upon literature to illuminate the process of forgiveness. Using the work of Sue Miller, McAvoy explores not only theological issues present in forgiveness, but also the dynamics and role of such aspects as gender, power, and memory. Her article provides insight by examining the narratives of characters in the novel and exploring them in light of the forgiveness process.

We decided to use two fictional pieces in this issue realizing that some of the subtleties and complexities of forgiveness may best be addressed in fiction. Marilyn Born's "Three Spirits: One Parish," tells the story of a victim/survivor of abuse and makes clear the interconnection of individuals and their stories and the ripples of consequence that stretch far beyond the actual incidents of abuse. Nancy Poling's "When Sisters Dream," is a retelling of the story of Joseph in Hebrew Scriptures but with female characters. Using this device, she explores the particular meaning of forgiveness within family.

In this special volume, we have drawn from the breadth of religious studies to explore texts and teaching, theology and ethics, literature and fiction, research and theory, commentary and prayer, as they all relate to the experience of forgiveness in the face of trauma and abuse. We hope that this multifaceted approach will speak in some substantive way to you as a reader.

Forgiving the Unforgivable?
Jewish Insights into Repentance
and Forgiveness

Rabbi Mark Dratch

SUMMARY. Forgiveness, a beautiful, virtuous and honorable theological concept has, at times, been a stumbling block to healing and justice for victims, and has colluded, albeit unintentionally, in perpetuating the scars of violence and creating a few of its own. This article surveys traditional Jewish views of forgiveness and repentance. It defines these concepts and elucidates the need for reconciliation, reparations, healing and justice as prerequisites for forgiveness. *[Article copies available for a fee from The Haworth Document Delivery Service: 1-800-HAWORTH. E-mail address: <docdelivery@haworthpress.com> Website: <http://www.HaworthPress.com> © 2002 by The Haworth Press, Inc. All rights reserved.]*

KEYWORDS. Judaism, domestic violence, forgiveness, repentance

THE PROBLEM

Victims of domestic violence travel a long and arduous road toward achieving justice and realizing healing for the physical, psychological, emotional and spiritual wounds foisted upon them by their attackers. For many, the destination

[Haworth co-indexing entry note]: "Forgiving the Unforgivable? Jewish Insights into Repentance and Forgiveness." Dratch, Rabbi Mark. Co-published simultaneously in Journal of Religion & Abuse (The Haworth Pastoral Press, an imprint of The Haworth Press, Inc.) Vol. 4, No. 4, 2002, pp. 7-24; and: *Forgiveness and Abuse: Jewish and Christian Reflections* (ed: Marie M. Fortune, and Joretta L. Marshall) The Haworth Pastoral Press, an imprint of The Haworth Press, Inc., 2002, pp. 7-24. Single or multiple copies of this article are available for a fee from The Haworth Document Delivery Service [1-800-HAWORTH, 9:00 a.m. - 5:00 p.m. (EST). E-mail address: docdelivery@haworthpress.com].

is arrived at successfully. For many others, it is never reached. For yet others, the path itself is fraught with pitfalls, dangers, and further abuse by the systems and people that are there to help them. Religions and religious systems, ostensibly havens of comfort and protection, have at times failed their flocks because of personal and professional limitations of their clergy, the deficiencies in the attitudes and opinions of their communities, and sometimes through the well intentioned demands of their faiths. The issue of forgiveness is a case in point. What is a beautiful, decent and honorable theological concept has, at times, been a stumbling block to healing and justice for victims, and has colluded, albeit unintentionally, in perpetuating the scars of violence and creating a few of its own.

What is a Jewish view of forgiveness? What role does forgiveness play in the healing process of a victim? And what is its relationship to repentance, the obligation of offenders to make restitution, to transform their characters, to heal the wounds they created and to mend their relationship with their victims and with their God?

In order to formulate a Jewish response, we must cull the various and complex texts of Jewish law for their insights and attitudes. Briefly, this literature can be divided into two groups: the Written Law and the Oral Law. The Written Law is constituted by the Torah (the Five Books of Moses) and the rest of Scripture, the Prophets and the Writings, with the Torah being the most authoritative and its 613 commandments (*mitzvot*) considered legally binding. The Oral Law contains regulations that can be traced back to Moses at Mt. Sinai, as well as rabbinic exegesis, analysis, interpretation and legislation that has developed throughout the ages. The first written record of the Oral Law is the Mishnah (completed c. 200 C.E.), and also includes the Babylonian Talmud (completed c. 500 C.E.), the *Shulhan Arukh*, (the 16th century Code of Jewish Law) and rabbinic commentaries and codes that continue to be written to this day, evaluating, analyzing and defining past positions and applying their values and principles to contemporary challenges.

THE FUNDAMENTAL NATURE OF FORGIVENESS

"Fortunate is one whose transgression is forgiven, whose sin is covered. Fortunate is the person to whom the Lord does not impute iniquity, and in whose spirit there is no guile" (Psalms 32:1-2).

Forgiveness is a divine gift bestowed to flawed, finite human beings who, by dint of their very humanity, fail to attain a state of perfection, "For there is not a righteous person upon earth, that does good, and does not sin" (Ecc.7:20). So essential is forgiveness for the very survival of humanity and of human society that it is one of seven things created even before the world was created,[1] as it is written, "Before the mountains were brought forth, before you had formed the earth and the world, from everlasting to everlasting, you are God. You return (note: the Hebrew word for return is the same word as repent) humans to dust; and say, Turn back, O children of humanity!" (Psalms 90:1-2).

According to rabbinic tradition, the gift of repentance and the formula for its attainment were revealed to Moses on Mt. Sinai as he pleaded for mercy for the children of Israel following the sin of the golden calf. The Bible records,

> And the Lord descended in the cloud, stood with him there, and proclaimed the name of the Lord. And the Lord passed by before him, and proclaimed, "The Lord, The Lord God, merciful and gracious, long suffering, and abundant in goodness and truth, keeping mercy for thousands, forgiving iniquity and transgression and sin, and that will by no means clear the guilty; visiting the iniquity of the fathers upon the children, and upon the children's children, to the third and to the fourth generation." (Exodus 34:5-7)

In describing the unfolding of the scene recorded in these verses, the Talmudic sage Rabbi Johanan explained:

> Were it not written in the text, it would be impossible for us to say such a thing; this verse teaches us that the Holy One, blessed be He, drew his *tallit* (prayer shawl) round Him like the prayer leader of a congregation and showed Moses the order of prayer. He said to him: "Whenever Israel sin, let them carry out this service before Me (i.e., read these passages containing the thirteen attributes of God's mercy), and I will forgive them.[2]

And Rabbi Judah added that the verse, "Behold I make a covenant" (34:10) recorded just a few verses later, indicates that the revelation of these thirteen attributes actually formed a covenant that guaranteed that the people would never be turned away without forgiveness. This formula is the central theme of the penitential *Selihot* prayers recited during the High Holy Day season, culminating with Yom Kippur.

Essentially, God is a forgiving God who desires the repentance of sinners. Three times a day during the daily prayers, Jews recite the blessings:

> Bring us back, our Father, to Your Torah and bring us near, our King, to Your service. Cause us to return to You in perfect repentance. Blessed are You, God, Who desires repentance.

> Forgive us, our Father, for we have sinned. Pardon us, our King, for we
> have transgressed. For You pardon and forgive. Blessed are You, God,
> the gracious One Who pardons abundantly.

This theme is repeated again and again throughout the liturgy. The rabbis even
saw divine kindness and mercy reflected in God's Name itself. The Tetragramma-
ton, YHWH, is used as God's Name when He manifests His *middat ha-rahamim*
(love, kindness and forgiveness), whereas *Elohim* is used to designate His at-
tribute of justice.

WHAT IS FORGIVENESS?

Three words are used in Jewish literature to signify forgiveness: *mehilah*,
selihah and *kapparah*. While these three terms deal with the same concept,
they are not totally synonymous, and their nuanced meanings will be helpful in
this analysis. The term *kapparah* is most familiar to a general audience as the
root of the name of the holiday *Yom Kippur*, the annual Day of Atonement, a
day of fasting, confession and penitence, in which sins are expiated. To a more
select group, the term *selihah* may resonate as the root of the name of the
pre-High Holy Day penitential prayer service, *Selihot*.

What do these words mean and what do they reveal about the nature and process of forgiveness? *Mehilah* is a technical, legal term that applies when the
lender of money forgoes or waives all or part of the debt another person owes
him. When applied to the consequence of sin, *mehilah* is the remission or cancel-
lation of the punishment and any of the legal consequences of the sinful act.[3] But
in the repentance process, *mehilah* alone is insufficient because, in addition to a
sinner's liability for compensating for the losses he caused his victim to endure
or for the prescribed punishment that he must bear, sin has other consequences.
It also damages and contaminates a sinner's soul and causes him to become
alienated from God, ("But because your iniquities have separated you and your
God" (Isaiah 59:2)). A sinner requires purification and the healing qualities of
selihah (forgiveness) as well. The great twentieth century sage and teacher,
Rabbi Joseph Soloveitchik suggested that *selihah* "is a process which cleanses
and sanctifies the metaphysical dimension of the personality."[4] The purification
and sanctification that results from proper repentance are reflected in Rabbi
Akiba's homily found in the Mishnah, *Yoma* 85b, records,

> Rabbi Akiba said: Fortunate are you, Israel! Who is it before Whom you
> become purified? And who is it that makes you pure? Your Father Who is
> in Heaven, as it is said, "And I will sprinkle clean water upon you and ye
> shall be pure" (Ez. 36:25) and it further says, "Thou Hope of Israel, the

Lord!" (Jer. 17:13. The word *mikveh* is a homonym meaning both "fountain" (*mikveh* or ritual bath) and "hope"), just as the *mikveh* renders pure the impure, so does the Holy One, blessed be He, render Israel clean.

And the Talmudic sage Rabbi Hama son of Hanina said "Great is penitence, for it brings healing to the world, as it is said, 'I will heal their backsliding, I will love then, freely.' (Hosea 14:5).[5] Further, Rabbi Levi said, "Great is repentance, for it reaches up to the Throne of Glory, as it is said: 'Return, O Israel, unto the Lord thy God' (Hosea 14:2).

According to Rabbi Soloveitchik, *kapparah* and *mehilah* are synonymous from the Torah's perspective. We will soon see that other authorities distinguish between them.

HOW IS FORGIVENESS ACHIEVED?

God has the power to grant unilateral pardon only for those sins committed against Him (i.e., ritual laws). Forgiveness for violations perpetrated against another human being is not initially in God's hands, but first requires compensation of the victims who themselves were the injured party, who themselves were violated, who themselves have claim to reparations, and who themselves need to be appeased before divine forgiveness is available. The Mishnah, *Yoma* 85b, states,

> For transgressions between humans and the Omnipresent, the Day of Atonement procures atonement, but for transgressions between one person and another, the Day of Atonement does not procure any atonement, until [the perpetrator] has appeased the victim.[6]

According to Rabbi Eleazar son of Azariah, the verse is read as follows: From all your sins before the Lord, (i.e., sins between God and people) the Day the Atonement procures forgiveness; but not for those which are committed not "before the Lord," but against another person, the Day the Atonement cannot procure forgiveness. God must wait until the sinner has achieved forgiveness from his fellow, and then and only then can He forgive that transgression. Clearly both pardons are necessary as the sin, a violation of a biblical commandment, violated both relationships, the one between the two people and the one that the sinner has with God.

In formulating this concept in his legal code, *Mishneh Torah*, the twelfth century philosopher and legal authority Maimonides[7] (known by the acronym Rambam, which stands for Rabbi Moses ben Maimon) writes as follows:

[The liability of] one who causes physical harm to another is different from who causes financial harm. For in the case of one who causes financial harm, once compensation is made, the damager achieves atonement (*nitkaper*). But, in the case of physical harm, even if the aggressor made the five payments,[8] it is not atoned (*mitkaper*) for him. Even if he offered [as sacrifices to God] all of the rams of Navioth,[9] it is not atoned (*mitkaper*) for him and he is not forgiven (*nimhol*) until he requests [forgiveness] from the victim and [the victim] forgives him (*yimhol*).[10]

In this statement, Rambam highlights the steps required in order to earn forgiveness by employing two terms: *kapparah* and *mehilah*. In this context, these words are not synonymous. In this formulation, *mehilah* (forgiveness) refers to the forgiveness an injured party grants to the perpetrator and *kapparah* refers to the subsequent atonement that a sinner achieves from God.

In order for an aggressor to achieve forgiveness he must first regret his actions, and then,

1. make restitution for the damage he caused, as well as pay any other fines that he may have accrued while sinning;
2. appease the victim and acquire his forgiveness; and then, and only then;
3. seek atonement from God through prayer, confession and other acts of penitence.[11]

MUST ONE FORGIVE?

An initial survey of traditional Jewish texts argues that for ethical and *halakhic* (Jewish legal) reasons, one *must* forgive. Consider the Mishnah in Ethics of the Fathers, 5:11, in which conciliation and appeasement are deemed pious traits.

[There are] four types of temperaments: easy to become angry, and easy to be pacified: his gain disappears in his loss; hard to become angry, and hard to be pacified: his loss disappears in his gain; hard to become angry and easy to be pacified: [he is] a pious man; easy to become angry and hard to be pacified: [he is] a wicked man.

The Talmud, *Rosh Hashanah* 17a, teaches that one who is forgiving of the sins of others is forgiven for all of his sins. This formulation follows the classical view of *middah ke-neged middah*, that we receive our just desserts and are dealt with in this world on a "measure for measure" basis, just as we deal with others. And so, the cultivation of a kind and sensitive disposition that is quick to be appeased and quick to forgive is desirable, reflects positively on the forgiver, and stands him in good stead in his own life.

The Talmud informs us that the prayers of the great sage, Rabbi Akiba, were answered not because he was intellectually greater than his colleagues, but because he was forbearing and forgiving.[12] And Rabbi Nehunia ben ha-Kaneh, when asked by his disciples to what merit he ascribed his longevity, replied that among other things, "the curse of my fellow did not go up on my bed with me." One sage explained that every night before he went to sleep, Rabbi Nehunia ben ha-Kaneh said, "I forgive all who have aggrieved me."[13]

Furthermore, the withholding of forgiveness is considered a mark of cruelty. The Mishnah, *Baba Kamma* 92a, states,

> Whence can we learn that should the injured person not forgive him he would be [stigmatized as] cruel? From the words: "So Abraham prayed unto God and God healed Abimelech." (Genesis 20:17)

And even if one is hesitant to forgive one who has transgressed against him, he must do so after being asked three times:

> Rabbi Yose son of Hanina said: One who asks pardon of his neighbor need do so no more than three times, as it is said: "Forgive, I pray thee now . . . and now we pray thee." (Gen. 50:17)[14]

These verses are recorded following the death of the patriarch Jacob. At that point, his sons approached their brother Joseph pleading three times for his forgiveness for having thrown him into the pit and selling him into slavery. This precedent is the source of this ruling. It appears that these three requests serve a dual purpose. One, they are a serious attempt to appease the victim and to restore his sense of dignity and self worth. And two, they are meant to humble the aggressor who must now appear, hat in hand, before the one he previously mistreated and victimized. Should the victim then withhold forgiveness, despite the sincere and genuine petitions of the wrongdoer, he, the victim, then becomes guilty of debasing the petitioner and is deemed cruel.

PERMISSION TO WITHHOLD FORGIVENESS

But the granting of forgiveness is neither inevitable nor automatic, even if the sinner entreats his victim three times. Forgiveness must be deserved, and it is earned only after a victim has received restitution and has been appeased. The righting of wrongs and the exacting of justice are prerequisites for achieving forgiveness.

Despite the sources that call upon victims to forgive readily, liberally and eagerly, most Jewish authorities are of the opinion that there is no absolute obligation to forgive in all circumstances. Let us reconsider the Mishnah quoted above:

> Whence can we learn that should the injured person not forgive him he would be [stigmatized as] cruel? From the words: "So Abraham prayed unto God and God healed Abimelech."

A careful reading of this text indicates that there is no *legal* obligation to absolve another for a transgression. Note that the proof text comes from a narrative part of the Bible, not from a legal one, indicating an attitude and not an obligation. Further, the Mishnah suggests that one who withholds absolution might be considered to be cruel–a critique that reflects upon his moral character–and not "wicked," a designation of his legal status.[15]

There are texts that support this contention that one is not necessarily cruel, even when refusing forgiveness. The Talmud, *Yoma* 87b, recounts how the great Talmudic sage Rabbi Hanina son of Hama refused to forgive Rav for over thirteen years!

> Once Rav started to expound portions of the Bible before the Rabbis, when Rabbi Hiyya entered. [In deference to this great rabbi] Rav started again from the beginning; as Bar Kappara entered, he started again from the beginning; as Rabbi Simeon the son of Rebbi entered, he started again from the beginning. But when Rabbi Hanina son of Hama entered, he said, "So often shall I go back?" And he did not begin his discourse again. Rabbi Hanina was insulted. Rav [sought forgiveness for slighting Rabbi Hanina and] went to him on thirteen eves of the Day of Atonement, but [Rabbi Hanina] would not be pacified. But how could [Rav debase himself by asking for forgiveness thirteen tims?] Did not Rabbi Yose ben Hanina say: One who asks pardon of his neighbor need not do so more than three times? It is different with Rav. (He goes beyond what the law requires; his humility and kindness refuse to recognize limits in such matters.) But how could Rabbi Hanina act in such [an unforgiving manner]? Had not Raba said that if one passes over his rights, all his transgressions are [forgiven]? Rather, Rabbi Hanina had seen in a dream that Rav was being hanged on a palm tree, and since the tradition is that one who in a dream is hanged on a palm tree will become head [of an Academy] he concluded that authority will be transferred [from himself] to [Rav]. [Rabbi Hanina] would not be pacified. [Rav eventually] departed to teach Torah in Babylon.[16]

Even nightly grants of absolution for all those who wronged him that day, like that of Rabbi Nehunia son of ha-Kaneh cited above and that of Rabbi Papa cited elsewhere,[17] was a *middat hasidut*, an act of piety, and not an obligatory one. Why else would he be praised for it and why else would it be cited as an unusual act by which he merited longevity?[18]

In addition, if one vows never to forgive another, that vow is binding. Now, had it been legally forbidden to withhold forgiveness, the vow itself would have been null and void as is any vow that attempts to nullify a biblically prescribed obligation.[19]

Rema,[20] in his gloss to the Code of Jewish Law, *Shulhan Arukh, Orah Hayyim* 606:1, rules explicitly that an injured party may withhold forgiveness if he does so with the intention of benefiting the offender. Such benefit may include enabling the aggressor to achieve a state of humility or helping him to see his evil ways.[21] Other commentators add that one may even withhold forgiveness for one's own personal benefit as well, as is seen in the actions of Rabbi Hanina quoted above who withheld pardoning Rav, thereby enabling himself to retain his position of leadership in the Academy.

Consider as well that the biblical Joseph never forgave his brothers for having sold him into slavery in Egypt. Despite their repeated request, "Forgive, I beg you now, the trespass of your brothers, and their sin; for they did to you evil; and now, we beg you, forgive the trespass of the servants of the God of your father (Genesis 50:17)," there is no record that Joseph actually forgave them. The biblical commentator Rabbeinu Bahye suggests that the brothers never made proper amends, never having appeased their brother Joseph, and therefore were undeserving of forgiveness.[22]

Another account of withholding forgiveness comes from the rather off-putting comment of Rabbi Eleazar, son of Rabbi Simeon, found in the Talmud, *Ta'anit* 20b:

> Once Rabbi Eleazar son of Rabbi Simeon was coming from Migdal Gedor, from the house of his teacher, and he was riding leisurely on his ass by the riverside and was feeling happy and elated because he had studied much Torah. There chanced to meet him an exceedingly ugly man who greeted him, "Peace be upon you, Sir." He, however, did not return his salutation but instead said to him, "*Raca*, ("good for nothing") how ugly you are. Are all your fellow citizens as ugly as you are?" The man replied, "I do not know, but go and tell the Craftsman Who made me, "How ugly is the vessel which You have made." "When Rabbi Eleazar realized that he had done wrong he dismounted from the ass and prostrated himself before the man and said to him, "I submit myself to you, forgive me." The man replied, "I will not forgive you until you go to the Craftsman Who made me and say to him, "How ugly is the vessel which you have made" "[Rabbi Eleazar] walked behind him until he

reached his native city. When his fellow citizens came out to meet him greeting him with the words, "Peace be upon you O Teacher, O Master," the man asked them, "Whom are you addressing thus?" They replied, "The man who is walking behind you." Thereupon he exclaimed, "If this man is a teacher, may there not be any more like him in Israel!" The people then asked him, "Why?" He replied, "Such and such a thing has he done to me." They said to him, "Nevertheless, forgive him, for he is a man greatly learned in the Torah." The man replied, "For your sakes I will forgive him, but only on the condition that he does not act in the same manner in the future." Soon after this Rabbi Eleazar son of Rabbi Simeon entered [the study hall] and expounded thus, "A man should always be gentle as the reed and let him never be unyielding as the cedar." And for this reason the reed merited that of it should be made a pen for the writing of the Torah scroll, phylacteries and *mezuzot*.

God wants the sinner to repent, as expressed in Ezekiel 18:30-32,

> Therefore I will judge you, O house of Israel, everyone according to his ways, says the Lord God. Repent, and turn yourselves from all your transgressions; so that iniquity shall not be your ruin. Cast away from you all your transgressions, in which you have transgressed; and make for yourselves a new heart and a new spirit; for, why will you die, O house of Israel? For I have no pleasure in the death of him who dies, says the Lord God; therefore turn, and live.

Nevertheless, despite God's desire for repentance, His essential capacity for mercy and His identification as a God of forgiveness, He Himself may withhold forgiveness at times. This is so when a penitent has not truly repented or if he uses the future possibility of penitence as an excuse to justify his illicit behavior, as the Mishnah, *Yoma* 85b, indicates,

> If one says, "I shall sin and repent, sin and repent," no opportunity will be given to him to repent.[23] [If one says], "I shall sin and the Day of Atonement will procure atonement for me," the Day of Atonement procures for him no atonement.

This source is most relevant in our discussion of the victim of domestic violence. An abuser is one who perpetuates a cycle of violence. His request for forgiveness from his victim is often less than real, or is only a temporary retreat from future violence that he will cause, and can be compared to the one who says, "I shall sin and repent, sin and repent." In such cases, there is no true repentance and thus there is no obligation upon the victim to forgive.

Forgiveness may also be withheld if a sin is so heinous or irreparable that it is simply unforgivable. The Talmud, *Sotah* 47a, posits, "Whoever sinned and caused others to sin is deprived of the ability of doing penitence." Rambam lists twenty-four conditions that either preclude repentance altogether or make it practically impossible to achieve.[24] Rema, in his gloss to the Code of Jewish Law, *Shulhan Arukh, Orah Hayyim* 606:1, rules that one who has maliciously slandered another need not ever be forgiven as he can never rectify the damage he caused to his victim and to his victim's family. And in the ethical treatise *Orhot Tzaddikim, Sha'ar ha-Teshuvah*, the author describes certain interpersonal violations for which it is practically impossible to atone. These include theft of objects of unknown ownership because it is impossible to perform proper restitution, the siring of an illegitimate child whose status can never be rectified, and compulsive and continuous violations of the same sin.[25]

The Talmud, *Hagigah* 15a-15b, records the story of Rabbi Elisha son of Abuyah, known as *Aher* (lit., the other), a prominent teacher and scholar and a leading light of his generation whose apostasy had a negative influence and devastating impact on his generation, and who was barred from ever repenting. When encouraged by his student, the great sage Rabbi Meir to repent, *Aher* replied, "Have I not already told you that I have already heard [a Heavenly Voice] from behind the Veil, 'Return ye backsliding children'–except Aher."[26]

Applying this principle to the victims and perpetrators of domestic violence it is important to note that the act of abuse is an ongoing, recurring behavior that violates the physical, emotional and psychological well being of a victim and, often, her family as well. Demanding that a victim forgive her abuser after one or even three requests by the perpetrators may, in fact, not only be unhelpful, but may further victimize the victim, denying justice and preventing the recovery and healing processes to progress and her self worth to be restored. Furthermore, abuse often impacts one's family, especially one's children, who themselves may be abused or become abusers. In such circumstances, reparations and healing may be unattainable and forgiveness may be impossible.

If a person feels compelled by family or friends, or because of perceived religious principles, to forgive a perpetrator when she is not ready or eager to do so, such a perfunctory pardon granted under duress is of no value whatsoever. The victim was never appeased, as is required by Jewish law. Healing has not taken place. Justice has not been served and no transformation of the character or behavior of the aggressor was secured. Since the abuser's repentance is incomplete, forgiveness is impossible. This is so even if a person received some sort of compensation or reparations for harm suffered.[27]

HOW DO WE KNOW IF A PERSON'S REPENTANCE IS SINCERE?

Forgiveness is relevant only after a person has sincerely repented. What is the measure of such repentance? The Talmud, *Yoma* 86b, suggests that penitence can only be ascertained if the sinner, finding himself in the same circumstances with the same opportunities in which he previously sinned, refrains from repeating his wrongful behavior.[28]

Further answers to this question can be gleaned from the guidelines used to determine the legal standing of witnesses in Jewish courts. Because Jewish law maintains that the testimony of one who is in violation of Jewish law is inadmissible,[29] it is necessary for the courts to establish standards to judge when one has sufficiently repented and can then function once again as a proper witness. The Talmud elaborates upon the repentance required of those engaged in illicit activities that bring undeserved or illegal financial gain such as dice playing, usury, pigeon raising, and trading in the forbidden produce grown in the Sabbatical year. In each circumstance, the sinners must not only compensate any losses they may have caused others to suffer, but must conduct themselves in ways that are straight and honest and must bend over backwards to prove their integrity and transformation in those specific areas in which they sinned.[30] Consider the case of a butcher who deceives his customers by selling non-kosher meat as kosher, "he who is suspected of passing non-kosher meat [as kosher] cannot be rehabilitated unless he leaves for a place where he is unknown and finds an opportunity of returning a lost article of considerable value, or of condemning as non-kosher meat of considerable value, belonging to himself."[31]

What are we to do when a person claims to have repented and we are not in a position to test that sincerity out of our conviction to protect innocents from becoming future victims? Because repentance is a private, personal matter, it is impossible for all intents and purposes for us to judge the seriousness, comprehensiveness or effectiveness of another's moral transformation. God alone has the ability to evaluate the sincerity of repentance, as He said to Samuel regarding His preference for Eliab as the future King of Israel, "Look not on his countenance, or on the height of his stature; because I have refused him; for the Lord sees not as man sees; for man looks on the outward appearance, but the Lord looks into the heart" (I Samuel 16:7). A human court cannot be certain about such private, intimate matters, it cannot judge another's thoughts and motivations, and must, therefore, be guarded in its approach, be suspicious of the sinner's transformation and impose upon him the prescribed punishment for any violation that he may have committed, regardless of his protestations of repentance.[32]

Furthermore, the above measures pertain only when the sinner himself initiates the process of repentance and not when he does so after having been

"caught" or because of external pressures and demands. If one engages in repentance because of outside pressures, the bar is raised and his new behavior
must meet an even higher standard.[33]

REVENGE, GRUDGES AND HATE

Other biblical prohibitions are relevant to this discussion as well. The Bible
states, "You shall not hate your brother in your heart; you shall rebuke your
neighbor, and not bear sin on his account. You shall not avenge, nor bear any
grudge against the children of your people, but you shall love your neighbor as
yourself; I am the Lord" (Lev. 19:17-18).

Is it possible that if a victim does not forgive an abuser that she violates the
prohibitions against hating a neighbor, taking revenge and bearing a grudge?

These prohibitions certainly sensitize us to the spiritual and ethical challenges
that victims face. The effects of abuse can certainly rock the foundations of one's
moral character, ethical balance and personal sensitivities. Feelings of hate and revenge are normal responses in these circumstances. According to Jewish law, since
an aggressor needs to pacify his victim and it is the victim's prerogative to withhold
forgiveness until asked three times or until appeased, it is obvious that one who
does not forgive immediately does not violate any of these prohibitions.

Furthermore, these prohibitions do not obtain when one has been victimized
personally. The consensus among the religious decisors is that the prohibitions
against grudge-bearing and revenge apply only in monetary matters and do not
apply when *tza'ara de'gufa* (personal affliction) is involved.[34] Others[35] do not
make this distinction.[36] However, it is evident that even these latter authorities
do not relate these other prohibitions to the withholding of forgiveness. They
reason that if these prohibitions were violated when forgiveness was withheld,
the Mishnah, *Baba Kamma* 92a, which states that one who does not forgive another would be stigmatized as cruel and brings as a proof text, "So Abraham
prayed unto God and God healed Abimelech" (Genesis 20:17), would have
stated that by withholding forgiveness the victim is in violation of the biblical
prohibitions against revenge and grudges and that he would be considered a sinner. Since the Mishnah does not do so, it is apparent that they are not linked. Furthermore, all authorities permit withholding forgiveness and even exacting
revenge in case as heinous and as irreparable as that of slander.[37]

Early 20th century authority Rabbi Elhanan Wasserman suggests that none of
these prohibitions obtain when "violating" them serves a positive purpose.[38] Among
other examples that he brings, Rabbi Wasserman argues that although in general it is
forbidden to hate, one is permitted to hate another if that other is an unrepentant sinner,[39] as it is written, "The fear of the Lord is to hate evil; pride, and arrogance, and

the evil way, and the perverse mouth, do I hate" (Proverbs 8:13) and "Do I not hate them, O Lord, those who hate you? And do I not strive with those who rise up against you? I hate them with the utmost hatred; I count them my enemies" (Psalms 139: 21-22). Thus, he concludes, that if the purpose of avenging a wrong is to exact justice or to teach the aggressor a lesson, otherwise vengeful acts are permitted as well.

However, Rambam's formulation in his code indicates that he disagrees and that one who withholds forgiveness does violate these strictures. In *Hilkhot Teshuvah* 2:10, he writes,

> It is forbidden for a person to be cruel and unappeased. Rather, one should be easily mollified and hard to infuriate. And when asked to forgive, one should forgive wholeheartedly and enthusiastically. Even if the aggressor maltreated him and sinned against him a great deal, one should not bear a grudge and not take revenge. This is the way of the seed of Israel and their proper hearts. But heathens of uncircumcised hearts are not this way; they maintain their wrath forever . . .

And in *Hilkhot De'ot* 6:6, he writes,

> When one person sins against another, [the victim] should not harbor hatred and remain silent . . . Rather, it is incumbent upon him to speak [to his assailant] and to say, "Why have you done such and such and why have you sinned against me [by doing] such and such?" as it says, "Thou shalt surely rebuke your fellow." If the [aggressor] repents and asks for forgiveness, he must forgive. The forgiver must not be cruel, as it says, "And Abraham prayed to God."

However, it is crucial to note that even Rambam requires full and sincere repentance as an indispensable prerequisite for the granting of forgiveness. Rambam would agree that one is under no obligation to entertain petitions for forgiveness and would not violate the prohibitions against taking revenge, bearing grudges and hating until true repentance, reparations and personal transformation have been achieved.

REPENTANCE, NOT FORGIVENESS

This analysis shows that the classical Jewish approach emphasizes repentance, not forgiveness. Thus, the burden is on the perpetrator to right the wrongs for which he is responsible. Justice must be served. Thus, perpetrators of violence against others must focus first and foremost not on their own spiritual or psychological welfare or on their desire for forgiveness, but, rather, on the physical, emotional, psychological and spiritual well being of their victims. They need to restore their victims to health and safety. They need to protect the safety and security of future, potential victims and keep them from suffering at their hands. They need to undergo treatments and therapies, if such are possible and effective, and they must be prevented from repeating their heinous acts. Society must be given the opportunity to seek justice and to rectify the wrongs that have been perpetrated against individuals and to prevent further violations of individuals and society as a whole. Then, and only then, is forgiveness possible.

Repentance is a difficult task. After all, how can one undo the past? Even if physical scars can be healed, and that is not always possible, how can one erase the memories and horrors that afflict victims years and lifetimes after they have been attacked? Perhaps that is the true mystery of repentance and forgiveness, when it is properly earned. Perhaps that is why sincere repentance is so difficult to accomplish and forgiveness is so difficult to achieve.

The Talmud, *Avodah Zarah* 17a, tells the story of one man's attempt to achieve forgiveness for a lifetime of debauchery. Using metaphor, the following talmudic account tells us of this sinner's many attempts fix the blame for his failings on external factors–society, nature, his parents–and his desire to place the onus of his moral transformation upon others.[40] Ultimately he learns that "the matter then depends upon me alone!"

> It was said of Eleazar son of Dordia that he visited every harlot in the world. Once, on hearing that there was a certain harlot in one of the towns by the sea who accepted a purse of denarii for her hire, he took a purse of denarii and crossed seven rivers for her sake. As he was with her, she blew forth breath and said: As this blown breath will not return to its place, so will Eleazar son of Dordia never be received in repentance. He thereupon went, sat between two hills and mountains and exclaimed: O, you hills and mountains, you plead for mercy for me! They replied: How shall we pray for you? We stand in need of it ourselves, for it is said, "For the mountains shall depart and the hills be removed!" (Isaiah 54:10). So he exclaimed: Heaven and earth, you plead for mercy for me! They, too, replied: How shall we pray for you? We stand in need of it ourselves, for it is said, "For the heavens shall vanish away like smoke, and the earth shall wax old like a garment" (Isaiah 51:6). He then exclaimed: Sun and moon you plead for mercy for me! But they also replied: How shall we pray for you? We stand in need of it ourselves, for it is said, "Then the moon shall be confounded and the sun ashamed" (Isaiah 24:23). He exclaimed: You stars and constellations, you plead for mercy for me! Said they: How shall we pray for you? We stand in need of it ourselves, for it is said, "And all the hosts of heaven shall molder

away" (Isaiah 34:4). Said he: The matter then depends upon me alone! Having placed his head between his knees, he wept aloud until his soul departed. Then a Heavenly Voice was heard proclaiming, "Rabbi Eleazar son of Dordai is destined for the life of the world to come! . . . Rabbi [Judah the Prince, on hearing of it] wept and said, "One may acquire eternal life after many years, another in one hour!" Rabbi [Judah the Prince] also said, "Repentants are not only accepted, they are even called "Rabbi!"

This unusual and powerful account relates how, in response to the cutting remark of a prostitute, Eleazar son of Dordai was moved to seek divine mercy. He looked to blame his behavior on external factors and forces. He concluded, however, that he alone was responsible for his behavior and his deep-felt remorse led to repentance and, ultimately, to forgiveness. So, too, in the situations under consideration in this article, abusers are the ones who are responsible for the violence they perpetrate. And victims have the right to justice. Abusers are the ones who must admit their wrongs, heal the damage they caused and transform their own lives. Clearly, we as a society have a vested interest in helping them in this path, both for their own good and for ours. But it is impossible to talk about forgiveness until, like Eleazar son of Dordai, the abuser acknowledges, "The matter then depends upon me!"

Our conclusion is clear. Repentance and forgiveness are essential to the human condition; without them, we are lost. Without them, people remain at odds with each other and sinners remain alienated and distanced from God. But forgiveness is not easily acquired. True repentance is a necessary and indispensable prerequisite for forgiveness, a state that must be earned and deserved. Repentance must rectify the abuses and damages of the past and heal the traumas to the emotional and spiritual well being of victims. Offenders must be sincerely contrite and do what is necessary to transform their characters and never repeat their offenses. Justice must be served. Then they may be worthy of true *mehilah, selihah* and *kapparah* and of the human and divine gifts of forgiveness.

NOTES

1. *Pesahim* 54a.
2. *Rosh Hashanah* 17b.
3. Pinhas Peli, *On Repentance: The Thought and Oral Discourses of Rabbi Joseph Dov Soloveitchik* (Northvale, NJ: Jason Aronson Inc., 1996), p. 270.
4. Peli, p. 271.
5. *Yoma* 86a.

6. This is based on an interpretation of the verse, "From all your sins before the Lord shall ye be clean" (Ez. 36:25).

7. One of the greatest Torah scholars of all time, Rabbi Moses ben Maimon (Rambam, Maimonides) was born in Cordova, Spain in 1138, and died in Egypt in 1204. He was a physician, philosopher and jurist. He authored a commentary to the Mishnah, the philosophical Guide to the Perplexed; *Mishneh Torah*, which summarizes the entire oral law concisely and in organized fashion; *Sefer Ha-mitzvot*, which lists the 613 commandments; and many responses.

8. *Baba Kama* 83b, One who injures a fellow becomes liable to him for five items: for depreciation of personal worth, for pain, for healing, for loss of time and for degradation.

9. Based on Isaiah 67:7, referring to the choicest flocks, and reflecting an attempt to achieve forgiveness through ritual, prayer and confession to God alone.

10. *Hil. Hovel u-Mazik* 5:9.

11. *Hil. Teshuvah* 1:1 and 2:2.

12. *Ta'anit* 25a.

13. *Megillah* 28a.

14. *Yoma* 87a; *Hil. Teshuvah* 2:9; *Orah Hayyim* 606:1.

15. This is not the case for Rambam who refers to one who withholds forgiveness as a *hotei* (sinner) and not just someone who is cruel. See *Hi.l Teshuvah* 2:9. (See *Bemidbar Rabbah*, par. 29.) Nevertheless, in 2:10 he refers to the withholder as cruel.

16. After the death of Raba, Rabbi Hanina became head of the Academy and he interpreted the dream to mean that he would die soon, to make place for Rav. In order to allow for another interpretation, with less fatal results to himself of that vision, he refused to become reconciled to Rav, forcing the latter to go to Babylonia, where in accord with that dream he did become before long head of the School of Sura.

17. *Megillah* 28b.

18. See Ritva to *Rosh Hashanah* 17a.

19. Responsa Rashi, no. 245. See also *Shevilei Leket*, II, *Hil. Nedarim u-Shevu'ot*.

20. Rabbi Moses ben Israel Isserles (Rema) was born in 1525 in Cracow, Poland, and died there in 1572 where served as head of the rabbinic court and yeshivah. His notes which reflected Ashkenazic halakhic practice were added to Rabbi Joseph Caro's *Shulhan Arukh*, which reflected Caro's Sephardic practices. Rema also authored responses and works about philosophy and Kabbalah.

21. *Magen Avraham, Taz, Mishneh Brurah*.

22. It is for this reason, he suggests, that the rabbinic tradition connects the subsequent deaths of the ten martyrs at the hands of the Romans as punishment for the sin of the ten brothers of Joseph.

23. Because this statement indicates that he never experienced genuine regret.

24. *Hilkhot Teshuvah*, ch. 4.

25. See also *Baba Batra* 88b, [In] what [respect], then are [the punishments for giving false measures] greater [than those for marrying forbidden relatives]?–There, [in the case of incest] repentance is possible, but here, [regarding false weights and measures] repentance is impossible. One cannot remedy the sin of robbery, by repentance alone. The return of the things robbed must precede it. In the case of false measures, it is impossible to find out all the members of the public that have been defrauded.

26. The Talmudic selection continues.

27. [R. Meir] prevailed upon him and took him, to a schoolhouse. [*Aher*] said to a child, "Recite for me your verse! (i.e., the verse which you studied today, the answer

thus obtained was considered to have the prophetic authority.)" [The child] answered, "There is no peace, says the Lord, unto the wicked" (Isaiah 48:22). He then took him to another schoolhouse. [*Aher*] said to a child, "Recite for me your verse!" He answered, "For though you wash yourself with niter, and take thee much soap, yet your iniquity is marked before Me, says the Lord God" (Jeremiah 2:22). He took him to yet another schoolhouse, and [*Aher*] said to a child, "Recite for me your verse!" He answered, "And you, that are spoiled, what do you do, that you clothe yourself with scarlet, that you deck yourself with ornaments of gold, that you enlarge your eyes with paint? In vain do you make yourself fair, etc." (Jeremiah 4:30). He took him to yet another schoolhouse until he took him to thirteen schools; all of them quoted in similar vein. When he said to the last one, "Recite for my your verse," he answered, "But unto the wicked God says, "What have you to do to declare My statutes, etc.?"(Psalms 50:16). That child was a stutterer, so it sounded as though he answered, "But to Elisha God says, [What right have to you to declare my statutes, or to take my covenant in your mouth?]"

28. Responsa Rashba, II, no. 278.

29. *Hil. Teshuvah* 2:1.

30. *Hoshen Mishpat*, ch. 34.

31. *Sanhedrin* 25b.

32. *Sanhedrin* 25a.

33. Responsa *Tuv Ayin*, no. 6.

34. *Hoshen Mishpat* 34:29.

35. *Semag*, prohibition 12; *Sha'arei Teshuvah* 38; *Hafetz Hayyim, Petiha, Be'er Mayyim Hayyim*, 8-9 based on *Yoma* 23a.

36. *Sefer ha-Hinukh* 241-242; *Hil. De'ot* 7:7-8.

37. Elyakim Krombein, "*Nekimah ve-netirah bimkom tza'ar guf,*" *Tehumin*, VI, pp. 292-304.

38. Rema, *Orah Hayyim* 606:1, *Terumat ha-Deshen, pesakim* 212.

39. *Kovetz He'arot, Yevamot*, no. 655.

40. *Pesahim* 113b. See, however, *Berakhot* 10a, There were once some highwaymen in the neighborhood of Rabbi Meir who caused him a great deal of trouble. Rabbi Meir accordingly prayed that they should die. His wife Beruria said to him: "How do you make out [that such a prayer should be permitted]? Because it is written, "Let *hatta'im* cease?" (Psalms 104:35) Is it written *hot'im* (sinners)? It is written *hatta'im* (sins)! Further, look at the end of the verse: "and let the wicked men be no more." Since the sins will cease, there will be no more wicked men! Rather pray for them that they should repent, and there will be no more wicked. He did pray for them, and they repented.

41. See R. Yonatan Eyebeshitz, *Ye'arot Devash*, sermon 3, p. 56a.

Forgiveness
and the Jewish High Holy Days

Marcia Cohn Spiegel

SUMMARY. Speigel focuses specifically on the Jewish High Holy Days reflecting on the meaning of forgiveness in the context of Yom Kippur. *[Article copies available for a fee from The Haworth Document Delivery Service: 1-800-HAWORTH. E-mail address: <docdelivery@haworthpress.com> Website: <http://www.HaworthPress.com> © 2002 by The Haworth Press, Inc. All rights reserved.]*

KEYWORDS. Forgiveness and Judaism, forgiveness and Yom Kippur

During the month preceding the Jewish High Holy Days, Jews spend time examining their behavior of the past year and asking forgiveness of those whom they have wronged.

However, for some people there is a dilemma. Are they required to forgive acts which may be truly unforgivable? Are there, in fact, acts which are unforgivable? Each fall as we approach the Days of Awe, victims of early childhood sexual abuse, and others who have survived psychological or physical abuse at the hands of those whom they loved and trusted may ask themselves these questions. They may never have reconciled with the perpetrator of the terrible acts

[Haworth co-indexing entry note]: "Forgiveness and the Jewish High Holy Days." Speigel, Marcia Cohn. Co-published simultaneously in Journal of Religion & Abuse (The Haworth Pastoral Press, an imprint of The Haworth Press, Inc.) Vol. 4, No. 4, 2002, pp. 25-27; and: *Forgiveness and Abuse: Jewish and Christian Reflections* (ed: Marie M. Fortune, and Joretta L. Marshall) The Haworth Pastoral Press, an imprint of The Haworth Press, Inc., 2002, pp. 25-27. Single or multiple copies of this article are available for a fee from The Haworth Document Delivery Service [1-800-HAWORTH, 9:00 a.m. - 5:00 p.m. (EST). E-mail address: docdelivery@haworthpress.com].

against them; the perpetrator may have refused to even acknowledge the abuse or may have died without ever taking any steps to make amends.

At the very time when we should be looking inward to examine our actions, and to make atonement to those whom we have wronged, the survivors of abuse may be overwhelmed by anger or resentment for the painful memories that continue to plague them. When memorial prayers in the synagogue encourage us to laud the virtues of parents or spouses who have died, these survivors may feel even more isolated and alienated from the very community to whom they turn for support.

Judaism teaches us that a person who has committed an act against another must go to that person to ask forgiveness, to rectify their behavior, to do tshuvah. While we are not required to forgive the wrong doer, we are encouraged to do so. Asher ben Yehiel admonishes us "each night before retiring, forgive whomever offended you." But how does one forgive the perpetrator of early childhood sexual abuse, or violence that has left us deeply scarred?

When we are struggling with flashbacks and nightmares and a variety of ailments brought on by the abuse, forgiving the offender may be far from our minds, or our ability. While we may not be able to forgive, we cannot continue to live with rage, fear and anger. Perhaps we need to find a word other than forgiveness in order to move forward.

Judaism has the concept of *shlemut*, wholeness, personal integrity and peace. Seeking *shlemut* may help us find our way toward recovery. There is also the concept of *shachrer*, to be free of, to be independent from, in other words to move beyond. When victims achieve *shlemut*, they may find the power to leave the abuse behind and move to a condition of *shachrer* to become survivors, even thrivers.

During the Holy Days we can use the prayers that speak of forgiveness as a time to draw deep into ourselves to begin to heal the pain. When we say kaddish, the memorial prayer, we remember that we are not praising the dead, but rather praising God who acts in this world. We can use this season to look at our own actions so that we do not use what was done to us as an excuse for what we have done to others. As we grow in strength and courage we may eventually be able to leave the past behind, and for some forgiveness may be possible.

This is a prayer of healing and renewal, offered in the spirit of Yom Kippur; was created by women and men in our community who have been deeply affected by abuse in Jewish homes and families. May their words strengthen our commitment to bringing about true shalom bayit (peace in the home).

O merciful and loving G-d, as we gather together in Your house on this, the holiest of days, we feel repentant, alive and deeply conscious of our past actions. We open ourselves to You as with sadness we face this truth: at times this past year we have acted cruelly. Some of us have abused our power and used control to hurt our spouses, our children, our parents. Others of us too often looked away, preferring not to see or speak out against abuse in our homes or in the homes of those we know and care about. We have been afraid to interfere.

Today, O G-d, we pledge that we will no longer allow injustice to reign in our homes or in our community. We will not stand by silently and will find ways to contain our rage and our need for power and control. In an effort to create change, we will seek counsel from our rabbis and other trained professionals. This year too, we will speak up on behalf of children who suffer sexual, physical and emotional abuse; we will not turn away from adults who live in fear of their mates; and we will reach out to help the elderly among us who are ignored or imprisoned in their own homes.

This day, O G-d, as we pray for renewal and redemption, we promise ourselves, each other and You that we will support shalom in all homes. May this year be different. Amen.

You have the right to be safe in your own home.
Abuse is never your fault.

Jewish Family & Career Services
Shalom Bayit Program
Atlanta, Georgia

Forgiveness and Mental Health:
An Exploration of Jewish
and Christian Approaches

Todd A. Heim

Mark S. Rye

SUMMARY. This study examined the relationship between forgiveness of others and mental health. It also explored Jewish and Christian approaches to the conceptualization and practice of forgiveness. Participants were recruited from several Midwestern US churches and synagogues. Participants answered self-report questionnaires concerning religiousness (religious affiliation, level of religious activity, Intrinsic Religiousness), situational forgiveness (Absence of Negative-AN; Presence of Positive-PP), dispositional forgiveness (Forgiveness Likelihood), conceptualization of forgiveness (Forgiveness Concept) and mental health (State Anger, Trait Anger, Hope, Depression, Existential Well-Being, Religious Well-Being). Consistent with hypotheses, after controlling for demographic/background variables, Forgiveness (AN) was positively correlated with Existential and Religious Well-Being, and negatively correlated with State Anger and Depression. Forgiveness (PP) was also positively correlated with Exis-

---

The authors would like to thank Dr. Kenneth Pargament for his helpful suggestions on an earlier draft of this manuscript.

[Haworth co-indexing entry note]: "Forgiveness and Mental Health: An Exploration of Jewish and Christian Approaches." Heim, Todd A., and Mark S. Rye. Co-published simultaneously in Journal of Religion & Abuse (The Haworth Pastoral Press, an imprint of The Haworth Press, Inc.) Vol. 4, No. 4, 2002, pp. 29-49; and: *Forgiveness and Abuse: Jewish and Christian Reflections* (ed: Marie M. Fortune, and Joretta L. Marshall) The Haworth Pastoral Press, an imprint of The Haworth Press, Inc., 2002, pp. 29-49. Single or multiple copies of this article are available for a fee from The Haworth Document Delivery Service [1-800-HAWORTH, 9:00 a.m. - 5:00 p.m. (EST). E-mail address: docdelivery@haworthpress.com].

Journal of Religion and Abuse, Vol. 4(4) 2002
http://www.haworthpress.com/store/product.asp?sku=J154
10.1300J154v04n04_04

tential Well-Being and negatively correlated with State Anger. Contrary to hypotheses, no relationship was found between dispositional forgiveness and mental health. No significant differences were found between Christian and Jewish participants on measures of situational or dispositional forgiveness. However, Christian participants were more likely than Jewish participants to disagree that one should only forgive after the offender expresses contrition. Study implications and limitations are discussed. *[Article copies available for a fee from The Haworth Document Delivery Service: 1-800-HAWORTH. E-mail address: <docdelivery@haworthpress.com> Website: <http://www.HaworthPress.com> © 2002 by The Haworth Press, Inc. All rights reserved.]*

KEYWORDS. Forgiveness, religion, Christianity, Judaism

Research generally suggests that forgiveness is positively related to mental health. Specifically, forgiveness has been shown to relate to greater hope (Al-Mabuk, Enright, & Cardis, 1995; Freedman & Enright, 1996), greater self-esteem (Al-Mabuk et al., 1995; Freedman & Enright, 1996), less depression (Freedman & Enright, 1996), less anxiety (Al-Mabuk et al., 1995; Freedman & Enright, 1996), less grief (Coyle & Enright, 1997), less desire for revenge (McCullough & Worthington, 1995), and greater existential well-being (Rye & Pargament, 2002). While these findings are promising, they need to be replicated using a wider variety of populations in order to help mental health practitioners better understand possible effects of helping clients to forgive. Furthermore, there is a lack of research examining how various religious groups conceptualize and practice forgiveness. Although forgiveness can occur outside of a religious context, for many individuals they are intertwined (Pargament & Rye, 1998). Mental health practitioners will enhance their ability to work sensitively and effectively with religious clients from diverse backgrounds if they understand their perspectives on forgiveness. Therefore, this study seeks to further understand how forgiveness relates to mental health and to explore how adherents of two religions (Judaism and Christianity) conceptualize and practice forgiveness.

DEFINITION OF FORGIVENESS

Forgiveness involves letting go of negative thoughts, feelings, and behaviors toward an offender and may include developing a positive perspective toward the offender (Rye & Pargament, 2002). Examples of engendering a positive perspective might include developing feelings of compassion toward the offender or praying for the offender. However, it should be noted that there is no consensus in the literature with respect to whether forgiveness necessarily involves engendering a positive perspective. Several authors have emphasized the importance of distinguishing between forgiveness and reconciliation because sometimes it is unwise or undesirable to reconcile with an offender (Enright & Zell, 1989; Freedman, 1998). In addition, forgiveness is different from forgetting, condoning, and legal pardon (Enright & Zell, 1989). An interesting question that has not received sufficient attention in the literature is whether developing a positive perspective toward an offender (Presence of Positive) has similar benefits to letting go of negative thoughts, feelings, and behaviors (Absence of Negative).

Religion and Forgiveness

In order to obtain a fuller conceptualization of forgiveness, it is essential to examine its religious roots. Pargament (1997) noted that religion contributes to forgiveness in several ways. To begin, religion "can lend significance to the act of forgiving" (Pargament, 1997, p. 264). Forgiveness within the context of religion reminds humanity of the need for divine forgiveness, the opportunity to live a spiritually based life, and the need to enhance relationships with others and God. Religion also provides theological justification and role models for the forgiveness process. Furthermore, religion seeks to humanize the offender by relating the offense to the victim's own shortcomings and fallibility (Pargament, 1997).

Unfortunately, the role of religion in forgiveness has received relatively little attention from social scientists. Of the authors who have examined the religious roots of forgiveness, most have focused on a Christian perspective (see Educational Psychological Study Group, 1990; Enright & Zell, 1989; Gassin & Enright, 1995; Jones, 1995; Jones-Haldeman, 1992; Pingleton, 1989). Relatively few authors have examined forgiveness from the perspectives of Judaism (see Dorff, 1998; Newman, 1987) and other religions (see Rye et al., 2000). Although forgiveness is valued by a variety of religions, this study will focus on how adherents of Judaism and Christianity approach forgiveness. These religions were selected because the researchers had ready access to these populations through local churches and synagogues, and mental health practitioners in the United States frequently encounter clients from these traditions.

Jewish and Christian Conceptualizations of Forgiveness

There are many similarities with respect to how Judaism and Christianity view forgiveness. This is not surprising given that both are monotheistic religions and Christianity has its roots in Judaism. To begin, both Judaism and

Christianity highly value forgiveness (Rye et al., 2000). Both traditions are similar with respect to the theological reasons for forgiveness (Rye et al., 2000). Specifically, God is viewed as forgiving the sins of humans who, in turn, are encouraged to imitate God. The Torah states that Jews are to be "walking in all His ways" (Deuteronomy 11:22), a directive that is rooted in the covenant between God and the Jewish people. Similarly, Christians are encouraged to forgive "each other; just as the Lord has forgiven you" (Colossians 3:13, NRSV). In addition, the sacred texts of both traditions contain numerous role models for forgiveness. An example valued by both traditions is the story of Joseph forgiving his brothers for selling him into slavery. For Christians, Jesus is an important role model for forgiveness.

Judaism and Christianity differ, however, with respect to the conditionality of forgiveness. In Judaism, once an individual offends another, the victim "must do everything possible to forgive the transgressor once the transgressor has gone through the process of return" (Dorff, 1998, p. 46). This process is called *Teshuvah*, and was outlined by the Jewish Rabbi Maimonides in the Mishneh Torah (Dorff, 1998). *Teshuvah* involves acknowledging the wrongdoing and then making a public expression of remorse to both God and the community. The perpetrator must also assert that he/she will not sin in this manner again. The offender then must offer compensation to the victim, and sincerely ask for forgiveness. The offender is to avoid the situations in which the offense occurred, and act differently when confronted with the situation again (Dorff, 1998). If the offender does not go through this process, victims may still choose to forgive so that they can move on with their lives. However, Dorff noted that in Judaism, "free" forgiveness is not encouraged, and the process of return is the preferred method of attaining forgiveness (as cited in Rye et al., 2000).

In contrast, the decision to forgive within Christianity is generally viewed as less dependent upon the offender's actions. The New Testament contains several examples of forgiveness that are unrelated to the offender's actions. For example, the parable of the prodigal son in Luke 15:11-32 depicts a father forgiving his son before his son shows contrition. In Matthew 18:21-22 (NRSV), Jesus tells Peter that he should forgive "seventy seven times." It has been suggested that Jesus meant that forgiveness should be a way of life (Jones-Haldeman, 1992), and no preconditions were mentioned. A possible exception might be Luke 17: 3 (NRSV) which states, "If another disciple sins, you must rebuke the offender, and if there is repentance, you must forgive." Although this could be interpreted to mean that forgiveness should be contingent upon repentance, many authors believe that Christian theology generally encourages forgiveness irrespective of the offender's actions. Lewis (1980) wrote, ". . . the uniqueness of Christian forgiveness, lies precisely in its unconditionality. . . Christian forgiveness does not require the repentance of the one who is to be forgiven" (p. 243). Interestingly, a study by Krause and Ingersoll-Dayton (2001) found that some Christians endorse forgiveness irrespective of the offender's actions, while other Christians believe that forgiveness should be contingent upon the offender's actions.

Understanding similarities and differences with respect to how religions view forgiveness is especially important for mental health practitioners who are working with religious clients who wish to forgive. However, one should not assume that adherents of religions necessarily conceptualize and practice forgiveness in a manner consistent with theological teachings. Research is therefore needed that empirically examines the attitudes and behaviors of adherents.

Empirical Studies Examining Religion and Forgiveness

Studies have shown that highly religious individuals value forgiveness more than individuals who are less religious (Poloma & Gallup, 1991; Rokeach, 1973). Similarly, Gorsuch and Hao (1993) found that those who considered themselves more religious reported more motivation to forgive than those who were less religious. They also found that Protestants were more likely to endorse proactive forgiving responses than Catholics, Jews, or those with no religious background. Although these studies are informative, more research is needed to explore possible similarities and differences across religious groups with respect to the conceptualization and practice of forgiveness.

It should be noted that there are significant challenges when conducting research comparing religious groups. Religious traditions are extraordinarily complex, and denominational or subgroup differences within a religion may in some cases be greater than differences across religions. Ideally, studies comparing religious groups would use a large sample of participants that are representative of the myriad denominations or subgroups that exist within a religion. Unfortunately, this is not always possible and one must be careful not to assume the findings from less representative samples will generalize to the population of interest.

Present Study

The present study will further examine the relationship between forgiveness and mental health and the role of religion in forgiveness. Specifically, the following questions will be addressed: (1) What is the relationship between forgiveness and mental health (i.e., State Anger, Trait Anger, Hope, Depression, Religious Well-Being, Existential Well-Being)? It was hypothesized that both situational and dispositional forgiveness would be associated with better mental health (i.e., increased Hope and Well-Being, decreased Anger and Depression). It was also hypothesized that Forgiveness (AN) and Forgiveness (PP) would have similar relationships with mental health. (2) How does religious affiliation affect the practice of forgiveness? Because of the importance placed within Judaism on the offender's behavior subsequent to an offense, and the likelihood that some offenders will fail to express contrition, it was hypothesized that Jewish participants would be less likely than Christian participants to forgive a specific offender and to forgive across hypothetical situations when no information about the offender's actions subsequent to the offense is provided. (3) How does religious affiliation affect conceptualization of forgiveness? It was hypothesized that there would be many similarities with respect to how forgiveness is viewed by Jewish and Christian participants. However, consistent with theological teachings, it was hypothesized that Jewish participants would be more likely than Christian participants to endorse forgiveness only after the offender expressed remorse.

METHOD

Participants

Participants ($N = 90$) were recruited from several Midwestern synagogues and churches. Participants' religious affiliations included Judaism ($N = 32$) and Christianity (Catholic $N = 28$, Protestant $N = 30$). Among Jewish participants, 69% identified themselves as Reform, 22% as Conservative, 6% as Orthodox, and 3% did not indicate a specific subgroup. Among Protestants participants, 54% indicated they were Baptist, 43% indicated they were nondenominational, and 3% did not indicate a specific subgroup. Thus, many denominations/subgroups within Judaism and Christianity were not adequately represented in this sample. The ages of the participants ranged from 18 to 80 ($M = 46.7, SD = 15.5$). The majority of the participants were female (62%) and Caucasian (99%). Most participants indicated that they had some form of college degree (72%), with 26% having a graduate degree, 32% having a bachelors degree, and 14% having an associates degree. The remainder of participants (28%) indicated they had a high school diploma or less.

Participants were instructed to describe a situation in which they had been wronged and to consider this situation when completing situational forgiveness measures. Types of wrongdoing reported by participants were classified into the following categories: mistreatment by a friend or family member (50%), gossip/wrongful accusation (19%), verbal/emotional abuse (16%), lying (10%), rape/sexual assault (7%), physical abuse (6%), infidelity (6%), miscellaneous (16%), and no answer/no comment (3%). The percentages add to more than 100 due to participants indicating multiple forms of wrongdoing. Most participants (55%) reported that they were mistreated over four years ago. Other responses included: 0-4 weeks ago (4%), 1-2 months ago (2%), 3-6 months ago (4%), 7-12

months ago (8%), 1-2 years ago (9%), and 3-4 years ago (15%). Three participants did not indicate when they had been wronged (3%).

Measures

Participants were given a battery of questionnaires that addressed demo-
graphic/background information, Intrinsic Religiousness (Hoge Intrinsic Religious Motivation Scale), situational forgiveness (Forgiveness (AN), Forgiveness
(PP)), dispositional forgiveness (Forgiveness Likelihood Scale), forgiveness
concept (Forgiveness Concept Survey) and mental health (State-Trait Anger
Inventory, Hope Scale, Center for Epidemiologic Studies Depression Scale,
Spiritual Well-Being Scale). The measures are briefly described below.

Demographic/Background Information

Participants completed basic demographic information about age, gender,
race, educational level, and religious affiliation. Participants also rated their
level of religious activity on a Likert-type item ranging from 1 (*Not at all active*) to 4 (*Very active*) and indicated how many days per month they attend organized religious activities. These variables were used to describe the sample
and, when appropriate, as statistical controls.

Religiousness

Intrinsic Religiousness. Religiousness was assessed using the Hoge Intrinsic Religious Motivation Scale (Hoge, 1972). This questionnaire has 10
Likert-type scale items with possible responses varying between 1 (*Strongly
disagree*) to 5 (*Strongly agree*). Sample questions include "My faith involves
all of my life," and "Nothing is as important to me as serving God as best I
know how." In this study, Cronbach's alpha was .90. Higher scores on this
scale indicate increased religiousness.

Forgiveness

Forgiveness Scale. Forgiveness of a specific offender was assessed using the
Forgiveness Scale (Rye et al., 2001). This scale consists of 15 Likert-type items,
with possible responses ranging from 1 (*Strongly disagree*) to 5 (*Strongly
agree*). Factor analysis revealed a two-factor solution (Rye et al., 2001). The Absence of Negative factor (Forgiveness-AN) contains ten items regarding the absence of negative thoughts, feelings, and behaviors toward the offender. Sample
questions from this subscale include "I can't stop thinking about how I was
wronged by this person," and "I spend time thinking about ways to get back at
the person who wronged me." The Presence of Positive factor (Forgiveness-PP)
contains five items regarding the presence of positive thoughts, feelings, and

behaviors toward the offender. Sample items include "I wish for good things to happen to the person who wronged me," and "I have compassion for the person who wronged me." In this study, Cronbach's alpha for Forgiveness (AN) was .84 and for Forgiveness (PP) was .86. Higher scores on both subscales reflect greater levels of forgiveness toward a specific offender.

Forgiveness Likelihood Scale. The tendency to forgive across situations was assessed through the Forgiveness Likelihood Scale (Rye et al., 2001). The scale contains 10 Likert-type items on which participants rate the likelihood of forgiving in response to a variety of hypothetical wrongdoings. Possible responses range from 1 (*Not at all likely*) to 5 (*Extremely likely*). Sample questions include "Your significant other has a 'one night stand' and becomes sexually involved with someone else. What is the likelihood that you would choose to forgive this person?" and "You accept someone's offer to attend a formal dance. However, this person breaks their commitment to take you and goes to the event with someone who they find more attractive. What is the likelihood that you would choose to forgive this person?" In this study, Cronbach's alpha was .92. Higher scores on this scale reflect increased willingness to forgive across situations.

Forgiveness Conceptualization. The Forgiveness Concept Survey (Rye & Pargament, 2002) was used to assess participant conceptualizations of forgiveness. The scale consists of ten Likert-type items, with responses ranging from 1 (*Strongly agree*) to 5 (*Strongly disagree*). Sample items include, "Forgiveness involves forgetting about how you were wronged," and "Forgiveness involves suppressing the fact that you are angry." For purposes of this study, items were not combined into a scale but instead were analyzed separately. This enabled researchers to compare Jewish and Christian participants on specific conceptual issues. Lower scores on items reflect increased agreement with the item statements.

Mental Health

Anger. The State-Trait Anger Inventory was used to assess anger (Spielberger, Jacobs, Russell, & Crane, 1983). This measure consists of two subscales (10 items each) measuring State Anger and Trait Anger. Items on the State Anger scale were constructed using a Likert-type scale, with response possibilities ranging between 1 (*Not at all*) and 4 (*Very much so*). Sample questions from this subscale include "I am mad," and "I feel like yelling at somebody." Responses on the Trait Anger scale range from 1 (*Almost never*) to 4 (*Almost always*). Sample items include " I have a fiery temper, " and "When I get frustrated, I feel like hitting someone." In this study, Cronbach's alpha for State Anger was .91 and for Trait Anger was .78. Higher scores on this scale indicate higher levels of anger.

Hope. Hope was assessed with the Hope Scale (Snyder et al., 1991). This measure consists of eight Likert-type items, with possible responses ranging from 1 (*Definitely false*) to 4 (*Definitely true*). Sample questions include, "There are lots of ways around any problem," and "I meet the goals that I set for myself." In this study, Cronbach's alpha was .83. Higher scores on this scale indicate greater levels of hope.

Depression. The Center for Epidemiologic Studies Depression Scale was used to measure depression (Radloff, 1977). This survey consists of 20 Likert-type items, with response possibilities ranging from 1 (*Rarely or none of the time*) to 4 (*Most or all of the time*). Sample questions include, "I felt that everything I did was an effort," and "I could not get 'going.' " In this study, Cronbach's alpha was .69. Higher scores on this scale reflect increased depression.

Spiritual Well-Being. Spiritual well-being was measured using the Spiritual Well-Being Scale (Ellison, 1983). This questionnaire consists of 20 Likert-type items, which range from 1 (*Strongly disagree*) to 6 (*Strongly agree*). The questionnaire contains an Existential Well-Being subscale (10 items) and a Religious Well-Being subscale (10 items). Sample items from the Existential Well-Being survey include, "Life doesn't have much meaning," and "I believe there is some real purpose for my life." Sample items from the Religious Well-Being subscale include, "I believe that God is concerned about my problems," and "I have a personally meaningful relationship with God." Cronbach's alpha in this study for Religious Well-Being was .93 and Existential Well-Being Scale was .80. Higher scores on both subscales reflect increased well-being.

Procedure

Participants were recruited from several Indiana, Michigan, and Ohio synagogues and churches. These institutions were identified through personal contacts of the researchers and by looking through the phonebook. Members of the clergy from each organization were initially contacted by phone and, after a brief explanation of the study, were asked if they would be willing to distribute questionnaires to members of their organization. Questionnaires were delivered to clergy members either in person or through the mail. The clergy then distributed the questionnaire to members of their congregations. Participants were instructed to fill out the questionnaire and either mail it directly to the experimenter or return it in a sealed envelope to their clergy leader, who subsequently mailed surveys.

Individuals were eligible for participation if they: (1) were affiliated with Judaism or Christianity, (2) were at least 18 years of age, and (3) had experienced some form of wrongdoing. No specific type of wrongdoing was required in order to be eligible for participation. Regardless of the nature of the offense, forgiveness was a considered a relevant response if the participant perceived that a wrongdoing had occurred. As mentioned earlier, participants reported a range of types of offenses. Of the 345 questionnaires that were distributed, 98 (28%) were returned. Thirty-four were returned from Jewish participants and 64 from Christian participants. Questionnaires from eight participants (2 Jewish, 6 Christian) were dropped from the analyses because they indicated they had never been wronged. Therefore, a total of 90 participants were included in the sample.

Each questionnaire was assigned a research code in order to preserve confidentiality. Additionally, participants were randomly assigned to complete one of two versions of the questionnaire. The versions differed only with respect to the ordering of measures. Both versions included demographic and religiousness questions at the beginning. The first version placed forgiveness measures before the mental health measures and the second version placed mental health measures before the forgiveness measures. This was done to minimize the possibility that results would be affected by how measures were ordered.

RESULTS

Preliminary Analyses

As shown in Table 1, means, standard deviations, and Cronbach alphas were computed for religiousness, forgiveness, and mental health measures. Cronbach alphas across measures ranged from .69 to .93. Correlations computed between mental health measures were generally in the expected direction (absolute value of r's ranged from .01 to .50). Correlations were also computed between situational and dispositional forgiveness measures. For-

TABLE 1. Means, Standard Deviations, and Cronbach Alphas for Intrinsic Religiousness, Situational and Dispositional Forgiveness Measures, and Mental Health Measures.

	Mean	Standard Deviation	Alpha
Intrinsic Religiousness	38.55	9.25	.90
Forgiveness Measures			
Forgiveness (AN)	41.46	6.55	.84
Forgiveness (PP)	17.29	4.70	.86
Forgiveness Likelihood	29.57	8.80	.92
Mental Health Measures			
State Anger	11.72	3.76	.91
Trait Anger	16.70	3.95	.78
Hope	25.27	3.20	.83
Depression	37.04	5.17	.69
Existential Well-Being	50.18	6.72	.80

giveness (AN) was positively correlated with Forgiveness (PP) ($r = .50$, $p < .001$), and Forgiveness Likelihood ($r = .29$, $p < .01$). Presence of Positive was also positively correlated with Forgiveness Likelihood ($r = .46$, $p < .01$).

Relationship between demographic/background variables and mental health measures. Correlations were computed to determine the relationship between continuous demographic/background variables (age, religious activity, number of days per month participant attends organized religious events, Intrinsic Religiousness, amount of time since wrongdoing) and mental health measures. State Anger was negatively correlated with religious activity ($r = -.24$, $p < .05$). Trait Anger was negatively correlated with religious activity ($r = -.25$, $p < .05$) and positively correlated with time since wrongdoing ($r = .22$, $p < .05$). Depression was negatively correlated with age ($r = -.37$, $p < .001$) and religious activity ($r = -.32$, $p < .01$). Existential Well-Being and Religious Well-Being were both positively correlated with religious activity (EWB-$r = .21$, $p < .05$; RWB-$r = .26$, $p < .05$). Religious Well-Being was also positively correlated with number of days participants attend organized religious events ($r = .28$, $p < .01$), Intrinsic Religiousness ($r = .71$, $p < .001$), and time since wrongdoing ($r = .39$, $p < .001$). Continuous demographic variables that were significantly correlated with mental health measures were controlled for in subsequent analyses.

ANOVAs were computed to examine the relationship between categorical demographic/background variables (sex, education, religious affiliation) and mental health measures. Race was not included in these analyses because almost all of the participants were Caucasian. Education was significantly related to Hope ($F(3,86) = 2.79$, $p < .05$). Duncan contrasts revealed that individuals with a high school education or less scored significantly lower on Hope than individuals with higher levels of education. Religious affiliation was significantly related to Hope ($F(2,87) = 5.08$, $p < .01$), Depression ($F(2,87) = 4.74$, $p < .05$, and Religious Well-Being ($F(2,87) = 16.65$, $p < .001$). Duncan contrasts revealed that Protestants scored lower on Hope ($M = 23.82$, $SD = 2.72$) than Jews ($M = 25.91$, $SD = 3.52$) and Catholics ($M = 26.11$, $SD = 2.85$). Protestants also scored higher on Depression ($M = 39.31$, $SD = 6.60$) than Catholics ($M = 35.78$, $SD = 3.72$) and Jews ($M = 36.00$, $SD = 4.04$). Finally, Jews ($M = 42.12$, $SD = 10.99$) scored significantly lower on Religious Well-Being than Protestants ($M = 53.56$, $SD = 7.22$) and Catholics ($M = 53.25$, $SD = 7.73$). Categorical demographic variables that were significantly related to mental health were controlled for in subsequent analyses.

Comparison between Jewish and Christian participants on demographic/background variables. A series of t-tests were computed on continuous demographic/background variables to determine if there were any significant differences between Jewish and Christian participants. Jewish participants ($M = 55.13$, $SD = 14.38$) were significantly older than the Christian participants ($M = 41.93$, $SD = 14.12$) ($t(87) = 4.20$, $p < .001$). Christian participants also scored higher on Intrinsic Religiousness ($M = 43.20$, $SD = 6.24$) than Jewish participants ($M = 30.11$, $SD = 7.76$) ($t(88) = -8.72$, $p < .001$). Christian participants spent significantly more days engaging in religious activities per month ($M = 9.58$, $SD = 7.11$) than Jewish participants ($M = 6.17$, $SD = 3.93$) ($t(85) = -2.88$, p < .01). Finally, the amount of time that had passed since the wrongdoing was higher for Christians ($M = 6.25$, $SD = 1.31$) than Jews ($M = 5.10$, $SD = 2.11$) ($t(85) = -2.71$, $p < .05$). Chi Squares were also computed to determine if there were any significant differences between Jewish and Christian participants on categorical demographic variables (sex, education). No significant differences were found. Consequently, age, Intrinsic Religiousness, number of days per month engaged in religious activities, and time since wrongdoing were controlled for in subsequent analyses comparing Jewish and Christian participants.

Analyses of Major Study Questions

Relationship between forgiveness and mental health after controlling for demographic/background variables. Partial correlations were computed to examine the relationship between forgiveness and mental health after controlling for demographic/background variables. As shown in Table 2, several signifi-

TABLE 2. Partial Correlations Between Mental Health Measures and Forgiveness Measures Controlling for the Effects of Demographic / Background Variables.

	Forgiveness (AN)	Forgiveness (PP)	Forgiveness Likelihood
1. State Anger[a]	$-.24^*$	$-.28^{**}$	$-.20$
2. Trait Anger[b]	$-.15$	$-.17$	$-.17$
3. Hope Scale[c]	$.17$	$.02$	$.15$
4. Depression Scale[d]	$-.32^{**}$	$-.09$	$-.15$
5. Existential Well-Being[e]	$.49^{***}$	$.25^*$	$.15$
6. Religious Well-Being[f]	$.31^{**}$	$.10$	$.12$

[a]Religious activity was controlled for in these analyses.
[b]Religious activity and time since wrongdoing were controlled for in these analyses.
[c]Education and religious affiliation were controlled for in these analyses.
[d]Age, religious activity, and religious affiliation were controlled for in these analyses.
[e]Religious activity was controlled for in these analyses.
[f]Religious activity, attendance at organized religious events, time since wrongdoing, religious affiliation, and Intrinsic Religiousness were controlled for in these analyses.
* $p < .05$. ** $p < .01$. *** $p < .001$.

cant correlations were found. Forgiveness (AN) was negatively correlated with State Anger ($r = -.24$, $p < .05$) and Depression ($r = -.32$, $p < .01$), and positively correlated with Existential Well-Being ($r = .49$, $p < .001$) and Religious Well-Being ($r = .31$, $p < .01$). Forgiveness (PP) was negatively correlated with State Anger ($r = -.28$, $p < .01$) and positively correlated with Existential Well-Being ($r = .25$, $p < .05$). There were no significant correlations between the measure of dispositional forgiveness (Forgiveness Likelihood) and mental health.

Comparison of Christian and Jewish participants on forgiveness measures after controlling for demographic/background variables. A separate ANCOVA was computed for each of the situational (Forgiveness-AN; Forgiveness-PP) and dispositional forgiveness scales (Forgiveness Likelihood), controlling for demographic/background variables, to compare the scores obtained by Christian and Jewish participants. Table 3 shows that no significant difference was found between Christian ($M = 41.45$, $SD = 7.47$) and Jewish participants ($M = 41.26$, $SD = 8.37$) on Forgiveness (AN) ($F(1,76) = .01$, $p > .05$). Similarly, no significant difference was found between Christians ($M = 17.68$, $SD = 54.92$) and Jews ($M = 16.48$, $SD = 5.52$) on Forgiveness (PP) ($F(1,76) = .72$, $p > .05$). Furthermore, Christians ($M = 30.58$, $SD = 8.01$) and Jews ($M = 27.89$, $SD = 8.94$) were not significantly different with respect to Forgiveness Likelihood ($F(1,77) = 1.39$, $p > .05$).

Comparison of conceptualization of forgiveness between Christian and Jewish participants after controlling for demographic/background variables. Separate ANCOVAs were computed for each of the ten items of the Forgiveness

TABLE 3. ANCOVAs Comparing Forgiveness Measures Between Christian and Jewish Participants Controlling For Demographic / Background Variables.

	Christian (N = 58) M (SD)	Jewish (N = 32) M (SD)	F Value
Forgiveness (AN)	41.45 (7.47)	41.26 (8.37)	.01
Forgiveness (PP)	17.68 (4.92)	16.48 (5.52)	.72
Forgiveness Likelihood	30.58 (8.01)	27.89 (8.94)	1.39

Note. Estimated marginal means and standard deviations are reported. Age, number of days attend organized religious events, time since wrongdoing, and Intrinsic Religiousness was controlled for in these analyses.

Concept Survey to determine if there were any differences between Jewish and Christian conceptualizations of forgiveness. Demographic/background variables were controlled for in these analyses. Bonferroni corrections were employed in these analyses to correct for the possibility of Type I error. Thus, the *p*-value required for significance in these analyses was .05/10 = .005. As indicated earlier, lower scores on these items reflect increased agreement with the statement. The results are presented in Table 4. A significant difference was found on question 6 (One should only forgive after the person who hurt you says

TABLE 4. ANCOVAs Comparing Means of Items on the Forgiveness Concept Survey Between Jewish and Christian Participants Controlling for Demographic / Background Variables.

Item	Christian *(N = 58)* M *(SD)*	Jewish *(N = 32)* M *(SD)*	*F* Value
Forgiveness involves forgetting about how you were wronged.	3.21 (1.56)	4.09 (1.74)	4.00*
When a victim of crime forgives his/her offender, there is no longer reason to prosecute the offender in a court of law.	4.27 (.80)	4.76 (.89)	4.77*
If we have truly forgiven a person who has hurt us, we should always seek to establish (or reestablish) a relationship with him/her.	3.22 (1.30)	3.55 (1.44)	.79
In order to forgive, we must be willing to overlook how we've been hurt.	3.08 (1.52)	3.60 (1.70)	1.45
Forgiveness involves suppressing the fact that you are angry.	4.01 (.98)	4.40 (1.10)	1.90
One should only forgive after the person who hurt you says that he/she is sorry.	4.05 (1.20)	3.05 (1.34)	8.47***†
Forgiveness usually occurs at a specific moment in time, after which all feelings of hurt and anger disappear.	4.15 (1.09)	3.96 (1.21)	.35
When someone is mildly annoying us, forgiveness is one possible response.	2.57 (1.30)	2.20 (1.45)	1.04
Forgiving others is usually an easy process.	3.87 (1.30)	4.16 (1.45)	.63
One can forgive organizations and institutions.	2.49 (1.32)	2.58 (1.46)	.06

Note. Estimated marginal means and standard deviations are reported. Items were constructed using a Likert-type scale with response possibilities ranging from 1 (*Strongly Agree*) to 5 (*Strongly Disagree*). Age, number of days attend organized religious events, time since wrongdoing, and intrinsic religiousness were controlled for in these analyses.
†Statistically significant after a Bonferroni correction was applied to correct for Type I error. The corrected p-value required for significance in these analyses was .05/10 = .005.
*p < .05 ** p < .01 ***p < .001

that he/she is sorry). Specifically, Christian participants ($M = 4.05$, $SD = 1.20$) were more likely than Jewish participants ($M = 3.05$, $SD = 1.34$) to disagree ($F(1, 77) = 8.47$, $p = .005$). No other significant differences were found after applying Bonferroni corrections.

DISCUSSION

The Relationship Between Forgiveness and Mental Health

Consistent with hypotheses, this study found significant correlations between forgiveness and several measures of mental health after controlling for the effects of demographic/background variables. To begin, both Forgiveness (AN) and Forgiveness (PP) were negatively correlated with State Anger. This is not surprising because forgiveness, in part, involves letting go of feelings of anger and hostility. Other researchers have similarly reported a negative relationship between forgiveness and anger (Glasner, 2002; Luskin & Thoresen, 1997, as cited in Thoresen, Luskin, & Harris, 1998; Rye et al., 2001). Mental health practitioners who are facilitating forgiveness with clients may find it helpful to introduce specific techniques for managing anger. In fact, several group interventions designed to promote forgiveness incorporate cognitive-behavioral techniques for anger management (Worthington, Sandage, & Berry, 2000).

This study also found a significant negative correlation between Forgiveness (AN) and Depression. Other studies using both correlational (e.g., Glasner, 2002) and experimental methodologies (Al-Mabuk et al., 1995; Freedman & Enright, 1996) have found a negative relationship between depression and forgiveness. Similarly, the finding that forgiveness measures were positively related to Existential Well-Being is supported by previous studies using both correlational (Rye et al., 2001) and experimental methods (Rye & Pargament, 2002). Although the mechanism by which forgiveness relates to depression and existential well-being is not completely understood, it is likely that cognitive processes play a role. Individuals who have difficulty forgiving often ruminate on the negative circumstances surrounding the wrongdoing. Similarly, depressed individuals often selectively attend to the negative aspects of their circumstances (Beck, 1979). Perhaps forgiveness involves a shift in cognition that affects one's mood and sense of well-being. More research is needed to explore this possibility.

A positive relationship was also found between Forgiveness (AN) and Religious Well-Being. As mentioned earlier, forgiveness is encouraged by both Judaism and Christianity. Individuals from these traditions who are having difficulty forgiving an offender might experience cognitive dissonance and a corresponding feeling of distance from their religious tradition. Perhaps forgiveness of an offender reduces such cognitive dissonance and thus enhances one's religious satisfaction and sense of connection to one's religious tradition.

The hypothesis that both Forgiveness (AN) and Forgiveness (PP) would be related to better mental health was partially supported. As noted earlier, both Forgiveness (AN) and Forgiveness (PP) were negatively related to State Anger and positively related to Existential Well-Being. However, it should be noted that unlike Forgiveness (PP), Forgiveness (AN) was negatively related to Depression and positively related to Religious Well-Being. Other studies have similarly found that Forgiveness (AN) is related to more measures of mental health than Forgiveness (PP) (Glasner, 2002; Rye et al., 2001). More research is needed to better understand differences between Absence of Negative and Presence of Positive. However, preliminary studies suggest that letting go of negative thoughts, feelings, and behaviors toward the offender may be the most important aspect of the forgiveness process with regard to mental health.

Contrary to hypotheses, Hope and Trait Anger were not significantly related to forgiveness of the offender or forgiveness across situations. In contrast, other studies have found forgiveness to be related to increased hope (Al-Mabuk et al., 1995; Freedman & Enright, 1996) and decreased trait anger (Rye et al., 2001). Perhaps the differences across studies can be partly explained by differing characteristics of samples across studies. It should also be noted that, unlike previous studies (e.g., Glasner, 2002; Rye et al., 2001), dispositional forgiveness was not related to mental health. However, the measure of dispositional forgiveness used in this study was originally intended for college students. It is possible that the measure did not adequately capture the types of wrongdoing with which older participants from the community are likely to be familiar.

Comparisons Between Christian and Jewish Participants

Contrary to hypotheses, there were no significant differences between Jewish and Christian participants with respect to situational forgiveness (Forgiveness-AN, Forgiveness-PP) or dispositional forgiveness (Forgiveness Likelihood). In other words, after controlling for demographic/background variables, Jewish and Christian participants were about equally likely to forgive a specific offender and to forgive in response to hypothetical offenses. However, Christian participants were more likely than Jewish participants to disagree with the statement in question 6 of the Forgiveness Concept Survey (One should only forgive after the person who hurt you says that he/she is sorry). The estimated mean score on this item for the Christian participants ($M = 4.05$, $SD = 1.20$) was on the

"Disagree" end of the Likert-type scale, whereas the mean score for Jewish participants ($M = 3.05$, $SD = 1.34$) was close to "Neutral."

Caution is needed when interpreting these findings. Importantly, the participants in this sample are not representative of the general population of adherents within the respective traditions. Most of the Jewish participants identified themselves as belonging to the Reform tradition. Absent from the sample was an adequate number of participants from the Orthodox and Conservative traditions. Within the Christian sample, both Catholics and Protestants were represented. However, even among Protestants, individual denominations differ significantly with respect to beliefs and practices. This sample did not include adequate representation from a variety of mainline Protestant churches. Furthermore, the response rate was relatively low and it is not known how, if at all, individuals who participated might differ from individuals who did not participate. Thus, it is unclear whether these findings are unique to this sample or whether they can be generalized to the respective traditions.

In addition, these findings are based exclusively on self-report measures. It is unclear to what degree, if any, differences might exist across traditions with respect to observable behavior. Some authors (e.g., McCullough, Hoyt, & Rachal, 2000) have emphasized the importance of including forgiveness measures that are based on observer report. Researchers should consider the possible role that social desirability might play in self-reports of forgiveness. For example, Batson and colleagues (as cited in Hood, Spilka, Hunsberger, & Gorsuch, 1996) conducted a series of studies suggesting that the relationship between intrinsic religiousness and prejudice may be influenced by social desirability. In other words, intrinsic religiousness may relate to lower self-reports of prejudice but not necessarily fewer observable acts of prejudice. Is it possible that a similar phenomenon occurs with respect to social desirability and forgiveness? Research is needed to explore this possibility.

An important variable that was omitted from this study, but which may affect forgiveness is lifetime history of exposure to trauma. Clearly, both the Jewish and Christian participants in this sample had experienced painful offenses. However, in addition to the individual offenses reported by Jewish participants, many Jewish individuals have experienced wrongdoings committed toward members of their entire religious community. It seems possible that memories related to the Holocaust and other painful experiences of anti-Semitism might be particularly salient to the older Jewish participants who were part of this study. Future studies should consider using history of trauma as a control variable. Mental health practitioners working with clients on forgiveness should attempt to understand how their client's decisions and perspectives on forgiveness may be affected by their previous personal or community experiences of wrongdoing.

Having made these qualifications, the possibility exists that Jews and Christians differ somewhat with respect to how they view forgiveness in the absence of contrition by the offender. As mentioned earlier, the Jewish tradition does not generally encourage forgiveness if the offender has not gone through the process of return (Dorff, as cited in Rye et al., 2000). An interesting test of this hypothesis could involve administering Jewish and Christian participants hypothetical vignettes depicting wrongdoing while systematically varying the description of the offender's behavior subsequent to the offense (e.g., contrition versus no contrition).

Implications for Mental Health Practitioners

In spite of the aforementioned limitations, the findings may be useful to mental health practitioners who are working with religious individuals who have been wronged. To begin, it provides further support that forgiveness of an offender is related to mental health benefits. These correlational findings, combined with the findings of previous studies using experimental designs, suggest that clients who value forgiveness and who wish to forgive an offender may benefit from mental health counseling that incorporates forgiveness. Further research is needed to determine whether there are certain client or situational characteristics for which forgiveness may be contraindicated. Furthermore, in cases of severe wrongdoing such as abuse, clinicians should be particularly sensitive to the timing of forgiveness. Our recommendation is that forgiveness should not be the focus of therapy when an individual is currently being abused. Instead, therapeutic efforts should be directed at helping the individual take action to enhance their personal safety. Once personal safety issues have been addressed, the practitioner needs to provide the client with an opportunity to express and process the painful feelings associated with abuse before exploring whether the client values forgiveness as a means of coping. Providing the client with education on the nature of forgiveness and how it differs from concepts such as condoning, forgetting, reconciliation, and legal pardon may be especially helpful. Premature encouragement of forgiveness or inappropriate imposition of forgiveness as a value may adversely effect the therapeutic alliance and the healing process.

This study also found a number of similarities between Jews and Christians with respect to the conceptualization and practice of forgiveness. Both Christian and Jewish participants scored similarly with respect to self-reported forgiveness of a specific offender and dispositional forgiveness. Clearly, adherents of both traditions value forgiveness. It is possible that Christians are more likely to endorse forgiveness in the absence of contrition by the offender. However, as mentioned earlier, this must be interpreted cautiously and future research is needed with large samples that are representative of the respective traditions. Also, it is unclear what, if any, differences occur with respect to observable behavior.

It is important to keep in mind that there are both individual and denominational/subgroup differences within each religious tradition. Consequently, mental health practitioners should carefully explore the values of their clients with respect to forgiveness and refrain from making assumptions based upon the client's religious affiliation. Mental health practitioners should also carefully explore how the client's history of personal and community trauma may influence their perspectives on forgiveness. Perhaps the findings of this study can provide a starting point for clinicians and researchers to further examine possible similarities and differences in religious perspectives on forgiveness among religious clients.

REFERENCES

Al-Mabuk, R. H., Enright, R. D., & Cardis, P. A. (1995). Forgiveness education with parentally love-deprived late adolescents. *Journal of Moral Education, 24*, 427-444.

Beck, A. T. (1979). *Cognitive therapy and the emotional disorders.* New York: Meridian.

Coyle, C. T., & Enright, R. D. (1997). Forgiveness intervention with post-abortion men. *Journal of Consulting and Clinical Psychology, 65*, 1042-1046.

Dorff, E. N. (1998). The elements of forgiveness: A Jewish approach. In E. L. Worthington (Ed.), *Dimensions of forgiveness: Psychological research & theological perspectives* (pp. 29-55). Radnor, PA: Templeton Foundation Press.

Educational Psychology Study Group (1990). Must a Christian require repentance before forgiving? *Journal of Psychology and Christianity, 9*, 16-19.

Ellison, C. W. (1983). Spiritual well-being: Conceptualization and measurement. *Journal of Psychology and Theology, 11*, 330-340.

Enright, R. D., & Zell, R. L. (1989). Problems encountered when we forgive one another. *Journal of Psychology and Christianity, 8*, 52-60.

Freedman, S. (1998). Forgiveness and reconciliation: The importance of understanding how they differ. *Counseling & Values, 42*, 200-216.

Freedman, S. R., & Enright, R. D. (1996). Forgiveness as an intervention goal with incest survivors. *Journal of Consulting and Clinical Psychology, 64*, 983-992.

Gassin, E. A., & Enright, R. D. (1995). The will to meaning in the process of forgiveness. *Journal of Psychology and Christianity, 14*, 38-49.

Glasner, D. E. (2002). *Differentiating between forgiveness of self and others.* Unpublished master's thesis, University of Dayton, Dayton, OH.

Gorsuch, R. L., & Hao, J. Y. (1993). Forgiveness: An exploratory factor analysis and its relationship to religious variables. *Review of Religious Research, 34*, 333-347.

The HarperCollins Study Bible (1993). New Revised Standard Version. New York: HarperCollins Publishing.

Hoge, D. R. (1972). A validated intrinsic religious motivation scale. *Journal for the Scientific Study of Religion, 11*, 369-376.

Hood, R. W., Spilka, B., Hunsberger, B., & Gorsuch, R. (1996). *The psychology of religion: An empirical approach* (2nd ed). New York: Guilford Press.

Jones, L. G. (1995). *Embodying forgiveness: A theological analysis.* Grand Rapids, MI: William B. Eerdmans.

Jones-Haldeman, M. (1992). Implications from selected literary devices for a new testament theology of grace and forgiveness. *Journal of Psychology and Christianity, 11*, 136-146.

Krause, N., & Ingersoll-Dayton, B. (2001). Religion and the process of forgiveness in late life. *Review of Religious Research, 42*, 252-276.

Lewis, M. (1980). On forgiveness. *Philosophical Quarterly*, 30, 236-245.

Luskin, F., & Thoresen, C. E. (1997). *The effects of forgiveness training on psychosocial factors in college age adults.* Unpublished manuscript, Stanford University.

McCullough, M. E., Hoyt, W. T., & Rachal, K. C. (2000). What we know (and need to know) about assessing forgiveness constructs. In M.E. McCullough, K. I. Pargament, & C. E. Thoresen (Eds.) *Forgiveness: Theory, research and practice* (pp. 65-88). New York: Guilford Press.

McCullough, M. E., & Worthington, E. L. (1995). Promoting forgiveness: A comparison of two brief psychoeducational group interventions with a waiting-list control. *Counseling and Values, 40*, 55-68.

Newman, L. E. (1987). The quality of mercy: On the duty to forgive in the Judaic tradition. *The Journal of Religious Ethics, 15*, 155-172.

Pargament, K. I. (1997). *The psychology of religion and coping: Theory, research, practice.* New York: Guilford Press.

Pargament, K. I., & Rye, M. S. (1998). Forgiveness as a method of religious coping. In E. L.

Pingleton, J. P. (1989). The role and function of forgiveness in the psychotherapeutic process. *Journal of Psychology and Theology, 17,* 27-35.

Poloma, M. M., & Gallup, G. H. (1991). *Varieties of prayer: A survey report.* Philadelphia, Trinity Press International.

Radloff, L. S. (1977). The CES-D scale: A self-report depression scale for research in the general population. *Applied Psychological Measurement, 1*, 385-401.

Rokeach, M. (1973). *The nature of human values.* New York: Free Press.

Rye, M. S., Loiacono, D. M., Folck, C. D., Olszewski, B. T., Heim, T.A., & Madia, B. P. (2001). Evaluation of the psychometric properties of two forgiveness scales. *Current Psychology, 20,* 260-277.

Rye, M. S., & Pargament, K. I. (2002). Forgiveness and romantic relationships in college: Can it heal the wounded heart? *Journal of Clinical Psychology, 58,* 419-441.

Rye, M. S., Pargament, K. I., Ali, M. A., Beck, G. L., Dorff, E. N., Hallisey, C., Narayanan, V., & Williams, J. G. (2000). Religious perspectives on forgiveness. In M. E. McCullough, K. I. Pargament, & C. E. Thoresen (Eds.), *Forgiveness: Theory, research, and practice* (pp. 17-40). New York: Guilford Press.

Snyder, C. R., Harris, C., Anderson, J. R., Holleran, S. A., Irving, L. M., Sigmon, S. T., Yoshinobu, L., Gibb, J., Langelle, C., & Harney, P. (1991). The will and the ways:

Development and validation of an individual-differences measure of hope. *Journal of Personality and Social Psychology, 60,* 570-585.

Spielberger, C. D., Jacobs, G., Russell, S., & Crane, R. S. (1983). Assessment of anger: The State-Trait Anger Scale. In J. N. Butcher & C. D. Spielberger (Eds.), *Advances in personality assessment* (pp. 161-189). Hillsdale, NJ: Lawerence Erlbaum Associates.

Thoresen, C. E., Luskin, F., & Harris, A. H. S. (1998). Science and forgiveness interventions: Reflections and recommendations. In E. L. Worthington, Jr. (Ed.), *Dimensions of forgiveness: Psychological research & theological perspectives* (pp. 163-190). Philadelphia: Templeton Foundation Press.

Worthington (Ed.), *Dimensions of forgiveness: Psychological research & theological perspectives* (pp. 59-78). Radnor, PA: Templeton Foundation Press.

Worthington, E. L., Sandage, S. J., & Berry, J. W. (2000). Group interventions to promote forgiveness: What researchers and clinicians ought to know. In M.E. McCullough, K. I. Pargament, & C. E. Thorsen (Eds.), *Forgiveness: Theory, research, and practice* (pp. 228-253). New York: Guilford Press.

Forgiving Abuse–
An Ethical Critique

Peter Horsfield

SUMMARY. This article argues that most Christian understandings and practices of forgiveness have lost the ethical framework that gives forgiveness meaning and makes forgiveness effective as a means of resolving the effects of abuse on individuals, communities and the abuser. From the context of a number of practical cases, it explores common Christian misconceptions about forgiveness, deconstructs common Christian practices, and offers a number of conditions that need to be present if forgiveness is to be recovered as an ethical action. The traditional Samoan practice of *Ifonga* is explored as an example of a communal and ethical means of redressing wrong within which forgiveness is embodied. *[Article copies available for a fee from The Haworth Document Delivery Service: 1-800-HAWORTH. E-mail address: <docdelivery@haworthpress.com> Website: <http://www.HaworthPress.com> © 2002 by The Haworth Press, Inc. All rights reserved.]*

KEYWORDS. Abuse, abuse and religion, forgiveness, reconciliation, clergy sexual abuse, victim, survivor, moral agency, ethical decision-making, sexual violence, pastoral care, Samoan religious practices, culture and religion.

[Haworth co-indexing entry note]: "Forgiving Abuse–An Ethical Critique." Horsefield, Peter. Co-published simultaneously in Journal of Religion & Abuse (The Haworth Pastoral Press, an imprint of The Haworth Press, Inc.) Vol. 4, No. 4, 2002, pp. 51-70; and: *Forgiveness and Abuse: Jewish and Christian Reflections* (ed: Marie M. Fortune, and Joretta L. Marshall) The Haworth Pastoral Press, an imprint of The Haworth Press, Inc., 2002, pp. 51-70. Single or multiple copies of this article are available for a fee from The Haworth Document Delivery Service [1-800-HAWORTH, 9:00 a.m. - 5:00 p.m. (EST). E-mail address: docdelivery@haworthpress.com].

In 1989 I became associated with a group of young women who brought a complaint of sexual harassment and abuse, in accordance with the formal procedures of the church, against a prominent church leader in Australia. Rather than implement formal disciplinary proceedings as the regulations required, the church leaders put the women's complaint in a drawer and proceeded as if a formal complaint did not exist. Instead, they advised the minister to resign from the parish and seek counselling.

The minister was allowed to announce his resignation to the congregation himself. He presented the reasons in vague terms as an act of faith in moving into an uncertain future. Though no longer minister of the parish, the minister continued to live in the parish, conducted weddings, visited people, served on church committees and represented the church on community bodies.

The women were invited to meet with the state committee responsible for dealing with complaints against clergy. The women responded, thinking they were giving evidence in support of their complaint. Unbeknown to them, however, many of the committee had not been made aware by church leaders that the women had lodged a formal complaint, and were acting on the basis that their purpose was to gather information to determine the type of counselling the minister needed.

The minister's sudden and unexplained resignation created grief and uncertainty in the congregation, leading to rumours spreading about the behaviour of "certain women" as being responsible. Efforts by the women to clarify what was happening to their complaint were fruitless. Eventually one of the women confronted the man in charge of collecting the evidence and elicited from him that the church had never recognised them as formal complainants. The church was not acting on a complaint, he said–they were simply counselling a minister with a problem. When challenged on this, he spat in her face the words, "You are wrathful women!"

Becoming aware of their disenfranchisement, the women lodged a second complaint, naming additional charges, this time with the support of two male clergy (!). On receiving this second complaint, the church leaders realised they could no longer keep it hidden and advised the minister to resign from the ministry. Formal disciplinary procedures that were required to be followed were delayed for several months to enable the minister to do so. The best the women and their supporters were able to do was force a minimal acknowledgement in the minister's resignation of the complaint laid against him.

Fourteen months after they lodged a formal complaint, the women received a letter stating that as the minister was no longer a minister of the church, no action could be taken on their complaint. Because the charges against the minister and his acknowledgement of them were never made public, the minister continued to serve as a church representative on a community ethics committee and was subsequently employed by another church body.

The congregation suffered immensely during this time, with responsibility for this damage being laid largely at the feet of the women. Two women were subsequently removed as elders of the church, one of whom had little knowledge of the complaint but objected to the manner in which it was handled in the congregation. All of the women left the congregation.

The support group formed by the women during this process–called SHIVERS[1]–remained active for a number of years. It was the first and one of the few support groups in Australia for adult victims of abuse and violence within religious communities. It provided support for a number of other women lodging complaints and a safe haven for women from around the country to share their stories of abuse and violence for the first time. Though having no formal recognition and no institutional support, its educational materials, community workshops, and lobbying activities were significant factors in churches in Australia beginning to recognise the reality of abusive clergy and lay leaders and belatedly adopting protocols in the mid 1990s to address the issue (though the protocols subsequently adopted were criticised by SHIVERS as inadequate in both framework and process).

I was one of two men associated with SHIVERS. My exposure to the trauma and injustice that results from clergy abuse through the group challenged the theological frameworks that up to that point had served me well. People as diverse as George Comstock (Comstock, 1976) in the area of social policy and Thomas Kuhn (Kuhn, 1970) in the area of philosophy of science have noted that people and societies do not dismantle their operating systems quickly or easily. The crucial factor for me was listening to the experiences of the women who crossed SHIVERS' path: experiences of abuse, violence and exploitation by religious leaders; and subsequent experiences of blame, ostracism and injustice as they sought to have those experiences recognised and addressed.

I came to identify this process of rethinking with Letty Russell's methodology of the theological spiral.[2] Within this method of theological construction, theological thought is seen as emerging out of an ongoing spiral of interaction, involving:

1. a commitment with those who are struggling for justice and full humanity;
2. a sharing of experiences of struggle in a concrete context of engagement;
3. critical analysis of the context of the experience;
4. producing a contextual examination of biblical and church traditions producing new insights;
5. leading to further action, celebration and reflection within an ongoing spiral. (Russell 1993, p. 31)

I became aware that a recurring theme in the experiences of many women survivors of sexual abuse and violence within religious communities is the pressure placed on them to resolve the situation "they were in" by forgiving the person who had abused them without any effort on the hearer's part to address the damage and danger that abuse involves.

I presented an address questioning interpretations and misuses of forgiveness at a National Resource and Training Seminar on Sexual Assault organised by the Royal Women's Hospital in Melbourne in 1993. The paper was widely requested and was reprinted the following year as an occasional paper (Horsfield 1994). I have received more responses to that paper than to anything I've ever written.[3] The response and the further stories that were written to me have confirmed for me that the ways in which the concept and practice of forgiveness is commonly constructed, communicated and interpreted within many Christian churches is misguided and inadequate for addressing the psychic, social and spiritual practicalities faced by women, and probably also for men, who have been sexually assaulted.

DOMINANT MISCONCEPTIONS ABOUT FORGIVENESS

There are a number of common ideas and practices of forgiveness that are challenged by the nature and experience of sexual assault.

One is that forgiveness is *the* Christian response to harm done by one person to another. Inherent in this is a strongly rationalist or cognitive expectation that a woman who has been sexually assaulted should be able simply to decide by an act of conscious choice to forget she has been assaulted and carry on her life as if nothing has happened.

Underlying this expectation is the theological belief that the grace of God or the power of the Spirit can override any human feelings or memories and in effect re-create a prior naivety or innocence. Commonly quoted when this expectation is made is the biblical passage: "So if anyone is in Christ, there is a new creation: everything old has passed away; see, everything has become new" (II Cor. 5:17). A woman who is "unforgiving" for whatever reason poses a threat to this belief.

Once one constructs forgiveness as a "good" and possible thing, a number of consequences follow. The woman's recalcitrance is frequently dealt with by attempting to change the woman's will by prayer, counselling, or even exorcism. If these don't work, the threat posed by the woman is managed by constructing her as deviant, vengeful or lacking faith or grace, commonly leading to her ostracism from the faith community.

This construction of "unforgiveness" as deviance can be subtle and sophisticated. A recent psychological-theological text on forgiveness presents an extensive treatment of what it called "grudge" theory, in effect an analysis of "the appeal and the potential (or perceived) benefits of holding a grudge" (Baumeister, Juola Exline et al., 1998). A further exploration of grudge theory in the same text suggests that unforgiveness may have a neurological foundation, a suggestion made on the basis of research of fear conditioning in rats (Worthington, 1998)! Associated with this idea are both secular and religious idealisations of forgiveness and reconciliation as *the highest aspirations* in situations of offence.

In Christian discourse, forgiveness is frequently presented as more than a personal responsive act, but as the proactive duty of every Christian as a means of partcipating in the mission of God. Commonly quoted in this affirmation is the Pauline passage: "All this is from God, who reconciled us to himself through Christ, and has given us the ministry of reconciliation; that is, in Christ God was reconciling the world to himself, not counting their trespasses against them, and entrusting the message of reconciliation to us" (II Cor. 5:18-19). Forgiveness in this discourse is seen not just as a matter of individual choice but as emblematic, as in the following: "Forgiveness is not merely one choice among a host of Christian themes . . . Forgiveness is rather Christian faith itself–whole, complete" (Barber 1991).

Forgiveness is at times given similar treatment in secular discourse as well, an ideal that by its idealism diminishes other responses to grievance. So,

> yet despite all the confusions which reduce forgiveness to amnesty or to amnesia, to acquittal or prescription, to the work of mourning or some political therapy of reconciliation; in short to some historical ecology, it must never be forgotten, nevertheless, that all of that refers to a certain idea of pure and unconditional forgiveness, without which this discourse would not have the least meaning. (Derrida 2001, p. 44)

A further misconception is the view that forgiveness is an effective tool for setting a victim of sexual abuse on the road to recovery from the effects of the abuse. As a consequence of this view, many women find themselves pressured to forgive their assaulter as a solution to their problems: long before they are ready and generally long before the wrong that has been done to them has been acknowledged and addressed.

A number of clinical psychologists in recent years have taken up this view of forgiveness as a unilateral therapeutic device, of concern only to the individual who has experienced the assault. In order to produce the effects, a number of writers have developed strategies for inducing an assumed state of forgiveness as a way of gaining its potential psychological benefits.

So Everett Worthington proposes what he calls a "Pyramid model of forgiveness," an "intervention program that has promoted forgiveness in people who have experienced hurts" (Worthington 1998, pp.107-8). The model is independent of any ethical or communal framework, and involves self-generated psychological actions such as (1) Recall the hurt; (2) Empathise with the one who hurt you; (3) Induction of a state of humility; (4) Make a public commitment to forgive; (5) Hold onto forgiveness. In this normative model, unforgiveness is understood as a psychological fear reaction producing negative responses: "The Pyramid Model of Forgiveness is based on an understanding of unforgiveness as a fear-based secondary emotion that motivates avoidance and revenge" (p. 132).

The "Learn Well Forgiveness Center," offers online courses and resources in forgiveness.[4] Courses include "Forgiveness therapy," "Forgiveness skills," and "Forgiveness Index." The five steps they propose are: (1) Acknowledge the anger; (2) Bar revenge; (3) Consider the offender's perspective; (4) Decide to accept the hurt; (5) Extend compassion and good-will to the offender. The effect of these, it guarantees, is "to release the offended from the offence."

What is characteristic of each of these is that, in a framework constrained by the four walls of the psychological consulting room, they ignore any ethical or communal dimension of responsibility in assault and place responsibility for resolving the effects of the assault solely on the individual who has been subject to the abuse.

A fourth misconception is that forgiveness is unconditional. It is to be given without any strings attached, irrespective of whether the perpetrator of the assault has acknowledged their wrong, irrespective of whether their abusive behaviour has been stopped so that others will not be similarly hurt, and irrespective of whether any process of remediation has taken place. The idea also emerges in Christian piety that forgiving an offender before any process of accountability is enacted, will cause the offender to change by the overwhelmingness of the love they're being shown by the person they have harmed.

Underlying this misconception is the theological view of the undeserved love of God as the motivation for Christian belief, devotion and practice. Theological echoes of the Augustine-Pelagian theological controversy over faith and works, and the Lutheran concern for salvation by grace alone, underlie the resistance to any attempt to suggest that there are conditions that need to be met before forgiveness is appropriate.

Though he acknowledges qualifications, Derrida sees this unconditionality of forgiveness as one of its essential characteristics:

> It is important to analyse at its base the tension at the heart of the heritage between, *on the one side*, the idea which is also a demand for the *unconditional*, gracious, infinite, uneconomic forgiveness granted to *the guilty as guilty*, without counterpart even to those who do not repent or ask for-

giveness, and *on the other side*, as a great number of texts testify through many semantic refinements and difficulties, a conditional forgiveness proportionate to recognition of the fault, to repentance, to the transformation of the sinner who then explicitly asks forgiveness . . . Must one not maintain that an act of forgiveness worthy of its name, if there ever is such a thing, must forgive the unforgivable, and without condition? . . . Even if this radical purity can seem excessive, hyperbolic, mad? (Derrida 2001, pp. 34, 39)

DO VICTIMS OF ABUSE RETAIN MORAL AGENCY?

A key issue in challenging these dominant ideas as misconceptions is the question of whether women who have first-hand experience of sexual assault are seen as agents of moral and theological discernment.

It seems at first to be a superfluous question–of course they do, most would readily argue. But when one listens to the stories of the ways in which women who are sexually assaulted or abused are subsequently treated, it becomes clear that *in practice* women who have been subject to sexual assault are frequently treated as though their personal testimony is no longer trustworthy, their judgment is impaired, and their insights questionable.

There are a number of deeply held cultural and patriarchal views about the nature of women's sexuality and the reliability of women's testimony that need to be explicitly challenged in order to identify the contribution that women's experience may make to a rethinking of the ideology of forgiveness.

Within the terms of Letty Russell's theological spiral (Russell, 1993), what if the authorities on what Christian forgiveness means and how it is to be practised are not the male theologians or philosophers writing from their privileged positions of tenure in city universities; nor the psychologists writing from their positions of professional detachment in comfortably paid suburban practices; but those women nurtured within the Christian faith over decades, who are then thrust into a real-life situation in which they have the first hand information for determining what is the appropriate Christian response to this situation?

What if, when women survivors of abuse say they are not able to forgive, they are not being weak, aberrant, or damaged, to be quarantined through prayer or counselling until they have recovered normality; but are reflecting a profound insight into the essential nature of Christian forgiveness. What if, in the terms of Letty Russell's theological methodology, their experience has given them a context by which to see that the common understandings of forgiveness reflected within churches are a patriarchal aberration of Christian theology that urgently needs correction?

If one takes seriously the context of women's experience of sexual assault, a critical deconstruction and reconstruction of the nature of forgiveness begins to take place.

DECONSTRUCTION

In addition to the misconceptions highlighted above, a critical view of forgiveness exposes a number of hidden agendas and motives.

One is that Christian forgiveness is often used as a way of avoiding unpleasantries. Much of middle-class western Christianity is about "niceness": constructing and maintaining an attractive community of friendly people as a basis for growing churches by attracting other people into a conflict-free shelter from a raging and at times threatening world. Quick forgiveness of "unpleasantries" helps keep Christian communities nice–quickly.

Church leaders often use forgiveness as a tool for settling abuse situations as quickly and easily as possible to avoid scandal, conflict and disruption to institutional programs, to spare them from having to confront or oppose a powerful and threatening person, to avoid possible legal action, and to avoid having to face up to injustice and abuse in churches' own structures.

Church members often put pressure on victims of assault to "forgive and forget" quickly because the assault makes them feel uneasy, they don't want to keep hearing about things that are unpleasant (once survivors of abuse and injustice begin talking, they can often want to talk about it a lot) and they find it difficult to handle the demanding emotional responses and the hard practical and faith questions those who have been assaulted begin to ask.

Women themselves may also want to forgive quickly for a number of reasons: as a way of bargaining for mercy and safety from the threat of their assaulter; to avoid facing up to the full vulnerability and implications of what has happened to them; because they feel that is what their faith requires them to do even though their bodies say otherwise; because they realise they risk ostracism from their own communities if they don't; and because they fear being labelled psychologically if they don't act according to expectation (e.g., behaving like a "victim" rather than a "survivor").

Therapists can urge forgiveness on clients because it seems to offer a way for the individual to deal with the consequences of an action when there are no supporting social structures of accountability, redress and restoration and affirmation of the person and their experience within a understanding community.

Christian theologians have a vested interest in promoting forgiveness because they see it as a central Christian doctrine (and, surreptitiously, as a central plank of an ideological framework and cultural institutional practices that justify and support their status). To say that women's experience of sexual assault gives the woman a distinctive moral and theological agency that may challenge the opinions of male theologians poses a threat to the established order of theological authority.

RECONSTRUCTION

Forgiveness, when genuinely given and experienced, and when the conditions are right, can bring liberation to both giver and receiver that is inestimable. However, I consider that much of our thinking and practices of forgiveness has been separated from an ethical framework that is essential if it is to have meaning. I suggest that Christian thinking about forgiveness needs to recover a number of emphases if its practice is to be meaningful, protective and effective.

The Recovery of Forgiveness as an Ethical Action

Much is written about the theological nature of forgiveness (Telfer 1959; Heyward 1987; Blumenthal 1993; Jones 1995; Muller-Fahrenholz 1996), and an increasing amount is being written about the psychological aspects of forgiveness (Simon and Simon 1990; Flanigan 1992; Dowrick 1997; Worthington 1998). But little is being written about forgiveness as an ethical concept.[5] Where it is, much of is so complex and abstract as to be of little use in determining whether forgiveness in any situation is an ethical action, and therefore an effective and theological one.[6]

By ethics I do not mean a legalistic framework. Nor do I mean a retributive framework that does not permit gratuity or grace. Ethos is the characteristic spirit, tone, beliefs, values and practices of a particular community that gives meaning and shape to people's lives. Ethos provides the framework for integration of the various dimensions of our experience into a meaningful individual and social identity. It is the ethos of communities to which we belong that generates shared hopes and commitments, that undergirds altruism and sharing, and that binds people together in trustful community relationships. Ethos is not necessarily a conscious thing: we carry it in our being–it shapes our identity, it reverberates in our emotional being, it sets the framework of health and sickness.

Ethics is the outworking of ethos in terms of practical rules of behaviour. It is a central aspect of the Christian ethos that inward faith ideas and experiences are expressed in outward moral behaviour. So a central part of Christianity is not just ideas but also corresponding ethical qualities such as respect, honesty, acting justly, acting with love, being fair, and honouring commitments, to name several.

The practice of forgiveness is more than just the psychological action of an individual: it is an individual action that takes its meaning from the ethos of the communities within which the person belongs. Along with pastoral theologian Don Browning, I believe that in our current situation, much of our thinking about what forgiveness is has become "unethical," i.e., separated from the ethos of its origins and from the communal context within which it has meaning. Browning writes,

> Without assuming the seriousness of the demand of Christianity for ethical inquiry and conduct, forgiveness loses its meaning and its renewing power. . . . It is only against the background of the tenacious concern to define in practical ways and with great attention to detail the meaning of the law that the gospel of forgiveness has power. (Browning, p.102)

Discerning whether one should forgive or not, therefore, involves consideration not only of whether it would feel good, solve some of my psychological problems, or make things easier. Determining whether to forgive or not involves discernment about the meaning of the offence within the ethos of the community: the individual and communal meanings of other actions that are available for responding to the offence; the individual and communal meanings of foregoing those other actions; and the individual and communal meanings of particular actions for my place and worth within the ethos of the community. So Jeffrie Murphy writes:

> Forgiveness is not always a virtue, however. Indeed, if I am correct in linking resentment to self-respect, a too ready tendency to forgive may properly be regarded as a vice because it may be a sign that one lacks respect for oneself . . . Forgiveness may indeed restore relationships, but to seek restoration at all cost-even at the cost of one's very human dignity-can hardly be a virtue. And, in intimate relationships, it can hardly be true love or friendship either . . . When we are willing to be doormats for others, we have, not love, but rather what the psychiatrist Karen Horney calls "morbid dependency." If I count morally as much as anyone else (as surely I do), a failure to resent moral injuries done to me is a failure to care about the moral value incarnate in my own person . . . and thus a failure to care about the very rules of morality. (Murphy and Hampton 1988, p.18)

I perceive that in many cases where survivors of sexual abuse are pressured to forgive, it has as much to do with reinforcing patriarchal subordination of women as moral agents, and expecting women to take their place, than it has to do with encouraging appropriate Christian action. In this context, withholding forgiveness may be a more ethical Christian action and should be encouraged by the wider community in favour of forgiving. John Stoltenberg in his book *Refusing to Be a Man* gives an instance of a young woman, gang-raped at the age of 14. "I forgave them immediately," she said later. "I felt like it was my fault that I'd been raped. I said, well, they're men. They just can't help themselves" (Stoltenberg 1989, p. 20). It is possible to imagine many Christian communities holding the woman up as a shining example of piety for her readiness to forgive. From an ethical perspective, however, to permit or support this young woman to forgive would be to support her view that she was of no worth and that men were not responsible for what they had done. Such unethical forgiveness would be an acquiescence and exploitation in the face of destructive evil. It would also reinforce a dangerous vulnerability in the young woman herself.

In similar vein novelist Joyce Carol Oates notes the important ethical function of forgiveness and unforgiveness through one of her characters in her novel *We Were the Mulvaneys*:

> Patrick said of Marianne she didn't know, or didn't want to know, when she was being exploited. She didn't know what evil was. She cheated herself of knowing because she forgave too soon. (Oates 1996, p. 266)

A consideration of the ethical implications of forgiveness and unforgiveness is beginning to be undertaken in the secular community in a wide range of social situations, such as Christina Montiel's analysis of forgiveness in socio-political situations (Montiel 2000), M. Kurzynski's analysis of applications of forgiveness in personnel management (Kurzynski 1998), Jacques Derrida's previously mentioned analysis of forgiveness in social and political situations (Derrida 2001), and Archbishop Tutu's *No Future Without Forgiveness* (Tutu 1999).

A number of writers on forgiveness, particularly within a psychological framework, make the point that forgiving an action doesn't mean condoning that action. However in practice this is generally interpreted as denoting internal attitude and perception–rarely are guidelines given by which to distinguish the difference between forgiveness as an action and its character as condonation. How does one distinguish practically between an act of forgiveness and an act of acquiescence to dominating individual and cultural damage and injustice? I would argue that not condoning an action needs to be expressed in the discernment of appropriate action, not just in intellectual assumption.

An ethical act of forgiveness needs to give attention first to crucial things such as whether the dignity and integrity of those who have been violated has been protected and restored; whether effective structures have been put in place for ensuring the safety and protection of other vulnerable people; whether there has been a clear affirmation of ethical expectations for fair relations between people of inequitable power; and whether legal and moral obligations have been met.

Set in this context, one should be alert to signals from survivors of assault that they cannot forgive. Baumeister et al., quoted earlier, would brand this as the woman holding a grudge, and would provide neuro-physiological arguments for her "weakness" in doing so (Baumeister, Juola Exline et al., 1998). But if one views forgiveness as an ethical issue, and women as moral agents, their action can be seen in a totally different light. It is not that the woman is holding a grudge, but rather that they take seriously the values by which we are urged to live. If these values are not affirmed or upheld by the broader community, the individual is placed in a situation where they cannot forgive without either denying their own worth or truth, giving in to the violence, denying the value of that which has been violated, or dehumanising their assaulter.

In contrast to so-called grudge theory, I consider the refusal to forgive may be seen equally as an individual's refusal to give in to the destruction of those with one of the only resources they have available to them: withholding of their approval.

Forgiveness Has Communal Dimensions, Not Just Individual Ones

A second crucial element is that forgiveness needs to be lifted out of an individual framework into a communal one. To a certain extent this is covered in affirming that forgiveness is an ethical concept, not just a psychological or theological one. An ethical framework affirms that actions are to be understood, not only in terms of individual effect, but in relation to the shared meanings that are constructed and nurtured within communities of interpretation. If an ethos is to mean anything, it needs to include processes whereby the values of the communal ethos are protected against behaviours that contradict them.

Within Christian communities of interpretation, leaders not only interpret the ethos of a community, they also represent it. When Christian leaders fail to act in situations of sexual abuse or violence within religious communities, they create a crisis of integrity. Abuse by a powerful person of others requires prompt, decisive and ethical action by other leaders to protect the integrity of the ethos by denouncing the abusive behaviour, affirming the value of those who were abused, holding the abusive person accountable, and restoring trust by restoring the fortune and rights of anybody who suffered because of the breakdown of the system.

Because it is largely an individual-oriented profession, psychological therapy tends to ignore the communal dimension of an experience such as abuse and deals with it within the terms of the effect it has had on the individual. Its focus is on the intra-psychic dynamics of the issue, dynamics that are accessible to the therapist–not redressing the communal betrayal aspect of the experience, which is beyond the bounds of the therapy session. Psychiatrist Judith Herman sees this a-ethical stance of psychological therapy as totally inadequate in responding to victims of sexual abuse:

> All the perpetrator asks is that the bystander do nothing. He appeals to the universal desire to see, hear and speak no evil. The victim, on the contrary, asks the bystander to share the burden of pain . . . Working with victimised people requires a committed moral stance . . . a position of solidarity with the victim. This does not mean a simplistic notion that the victim can do no wrong; rather, it involves an understanding of the fundamental injustice of the traumatic experience and the need for a resolution that restores some sense of justice. (Herman 1992, p. 135)

Psychological therapy has tended to see forgiveness as a device for psychological alleviation of symptoms rather than as an ethical issue. The basis on which healing is expected to take place is to help the person understand why this situation has happened, what its effects have been on them, and then working to dissolve those effects psychologically in individual therapy. Techniques of forgiveness are "taught" in order to achieve the alleviation of psychological symptoms.

In an ethical framework, sexual abuse is seen as a problem of the community. Sexual abuse is a situation in which one of the community members has been wrongly treated by another member of the community. Response to sexual assault therefore needs to address the issue communally: what does the community need to do to rectify this situation, to ensure that those who have suffered because of abuse within the community are given what they need to recover from that abuse, to have their fortune and place within the community restored, and to ensure that other members of the community are free from similar behaviour?

The importance of community is stressed as foundational to justice-making and forgiveness in the work of the Center for the Prevention of Sexual and Domestic Violence. But in my experience the failure to deal with sexual abuse communally is one of the major areas where survivors of abuse feel let down by their religious communities. Judith Herman among others notes that a crucial factor in recovering from abuse or trauma is to have the truth of what has happened recognised by one's community of reference, and incorporated as reality into the meaning and ethos of the community (Herman 1992, p.135). We do this in other situations such as good achievements, struggle, death-individual experience is responded to communally and becomes part of the shared life of the community. But in the case of sexual abuse, members of religious communities at times often go to extraordinary lengths to avoid taking a stance and giving the survivor's experience any opportunity for communal validation and support. Efforts are made to keep the survivor's experience individualised and to surround it with secrecy and suspicion–resulting in a literal shunning by her community and isolation at a time of greatest need.

It is in this context that we can best understand the comment sometimes made by church leaders that survivors of clergy abuse are never happy or that you can never please them. I don't believe that's the case. What I have observed, rather, is that people who were abused within a religious community expected quite rightly that the community would respond in terms of the ethos the community has been taught to live by. They are commonly shocked and disoriented to find that this doesn't happen. The problem here is not that survivors of abuse are hard to please–it is that the way in which the community and its leaders respond to abuse when it occurs is not in line with the ethos that is preached or taught.

The Issue of Power

A third area where thinking about forgiveness is deficient is in its failure to address sufficiently seriously the structural inequalities of gender relations within society, and between perpetrator and victim. In practice, this power imbalance results in expectations and the costs of forgiveness falling disproportionately on women.

The relative power of relationships between different people and different social groups becomes a powerful agent in how the issue is understood and the rules that apply to it. Power is central to understanding not only the mechanics, but also the meaning of sexual assault within our society. Jeffrie Murphy identifies this character of assault well:

> One reason we so deeply resent moral injuries done to us is not simply that they hurt us in some tangible or sensible way; it is because such injuries are also messages–symbolic communications. They are ways a wrongdoer has of saying to us, "I count but you do not," "I can use you for my purposes," or "I am here up high and you are there down below." Intentional wrongdoing insults us and attempts (sometimes successfully) to degrade us–and thus it involves a kind of injury that is not merely tangible and sensible. It is a moral injury, and we care about such injuries . . . Most of us tend to care about what others (at least some others, some significant group whose good opinion we value) think about us–how much they think we matter. Our self-respect is social in at least this sense, and it is simply part of the human condition that we are weak and vulnerable in these ways. And thus when we are treated with contempt by others it attacks us

in profound and deeply threatening ways. (Murphy and Hampton 1988, p. 25)

I contend that in general, people with power and resources within the society tend to resolve offences done to them by demanding recognition and obtaining justice and restitution. They support this action on the practical grounds that an uncorrected offence weakens their social stature and position and on the ethical grounds that if a person is allowed to get away with such wrong-doing, the moral structure of society will be diminished.

In general, those people within the community with less structural power and practical resources are required, even pressured, to resolve offences by forgiving them. To a certain extent this is because they lack the social power to muster community opinion in their support, and to muster community support in counteracting the tactical evasion of their offender. Judith Herman identifies how this social power works in assault situations:

> Genuine contrition in a perpetrator is a rare miracle . . . In order to escape accountability for his crimes, the perpetrator does everything in his power to promote forgetting. Secrecy and silence are the perpetrator's first line of defence. If secrecy fails, the perpetrator attacks the credibility of his victim. If he cannot silence her absolutely, he tries to make sure that no one listens. To this end, he marshals an impressive array of arguments, from the most blatant denial to the most sophisticated and elegant rationalisation. After every atrocity, one can expect to hear the same predictable apologies: it never happened; the victim lies; the victim exaggerates; the victim brought it upon herself; and in any case it is time to forget the past and move on. The more powerful the perpetrator, the greater is his prerogative to name and define reality, and the more completely his arguments prevail. (Herman 1992, p. 8)

In any situation of forgiveness, therefore, the process of ethical discernment needs to address seriously the relationships of power involved in the situation. The issue of discrepancies of power and their significance in resolution of abusive situations is well brought out in what is called the "Kairos document," a theological statement produced as a basis for action against apartheid in South Africa. Its statements about Christian stances towards apartheid may well be applied to stances towards other abusive behaviour:

> Church theology often describes the Christian stance of reconciliation in the following way: "We must be fair. We must listen to both sides of the story. If the two sides can only meet to talk and negotiate they will sort out their differences and misunderstandings, and the conflict will be re-

solved." On the face of it this may sound very Christian. But is it?

The fallacy here is that "reconciliation" has been made into an absolute principle that must be applied in all cases of conflict or dissension. But not all cases of conflict are the same. We can imagine a private quarrel between two people or two groups whose differences are based upon misunderstandings. In such cases it would be appropriate to talk and negotiate to sort out the misunderstandings and to reconcile the two sides. But there are other conflicts in which one side is right and the other wrong. There are conflicts where one side is a fully armed and violent oppressor while the other side is defenceless and oppressed. There are conflicts that can only be described as the struggle between justice and injustice, good and evil, God and the devil. To speak of reconciling these two is not only a mistaken application of the Christian idea of reconciliation; it is total betrayal of all that Christian faith has ever meant. (Kairos Theologians 1985, pp. 8-9)

Communal Forgiveness: The Samoan Ifonga

A good way to explore forgiveness as an ethical practice as discussed above is to look at the traditional Samoan practice of *Ifonga*. Though now significantly integrated into the more formal legal system, it illustrates a communal and ethical perspective on rectification and forgiveness. The outline of this practice as it was related to me is as follows.

If a member of a community offends a member of another community, the offence is handled between community leaders, not between the individuals themselves. This in itself involves a recognition that offence is a communal matter, not just a matter between individuals. The leader of the offending group goes personally and sits outside the home of the leader of the offended group, covering himself with an expensive fine mat–thereby hiding his individuality and embodying his representative office and practically humiliating himself in symbolic restitution of the humiliation that the offended people have experienced.

Members of the offended community are then given opportunity to express their emotions to the representative under the mat–rage, shame, embarrassment at the way they were treated. They are permitted to address the leader under the mat, including yelling, jumping on the ground, hitting the ground, but not touching him. Incorporated in the act of reconciliation therefore is a structured way for those who have been hurt to express the emotions that have arisen from the way they were treated, giving the people who have been most directly offended a chance to express their personal stake in the offence. In this way, the offence which has been done to individual people within the group is acknowledged and opportunity given for them to have the offence they have suffered communally affirmed, and their continuing value to the community affirmed and restored.

This expression of emotions continues until the leader of the offended group discerns that sufficient time has passed for the community to give voice to their emotional reactions to the offence that was done. For serious cases, the leader or community representative (who himself didn't do anything wrong) may be covered and subject to emotional harangue for days.

When the leader of the offended group has decided that emotions have been sufficiently expressed, he walks to the other leader, removes the mat (which he keeps as a gift of reconciliation), and invites him into his hut. Over kava (a drink of community) the two leaders discuss what other action is required to redress the wrong that has been done, determine if compensation is necessary, and restore bonds between the communities.

After the process is over, the leader of the offending community returns home. There he then takes his own action to remonstrate against and punish the individual wrong-doer, for whom he as leader is responsible, whose actions have brought the whole community into disrepute and caused the leader of the community such loss of face and humiliation.

It is enlightening to compare this communal response to wrong-doing, forgiveness and restoration to what is commonly experienced by women who are sexually assaulted by church leaders. Rarely does a person of leadership and authority within the church take on the woman's cause: the woman generally is required to handle the matter herself. Most bishops and superintendents have even tended to avoid being exposed personally to the experiences of victims of clergy abuse. This means they have little first hand experience with the real consequences of abusive behaviour on those who are the victims of it.

The primary focus of most bishops and superintendents has tended to be on protecting the interests of their institutions. Unlike as occurs in the *Ifonga*, most bishops or superintendents of offending clergymen accept no personal responsibility for their behaviour. In fact the opposite has often been the case–bishops and superintendents frequently go to extreme lengths to distance themselves from any responsibility for clergy under their jurisdiction. This has included in Australia Catholic bishops arguing legally, in contradiction of their theology, that priests do not represent the church. This may be legally pragmatic in the short term, but it fails to do justice and in the long term it has been seriously undermining the integrity of the institution and the fundamental teachings of the faith, leading to diminishing public respect and member loyalty. I believe in the long term it is also a more expensive way of dealing with the issue.

In contrast to the *Ifonga*, women who have been sexually abused within religious communities are rarely given opportunity to express the emotional impact of what has been done to them before the whole community. Likewise, congregations who have been betrayed by the actions of an abusive leader, are rarely given an opportunity to express the emotional responses that come with that betrayal. The expression of most emotions is tightly controlled in most religious community gatherings. Feelings of rage, embarrassment, disappointment, misunderstanding, betrayal, revenge or shame are rarely publicly expressed or dealt with. More commonly the woman is shunned by her community or she is pressured to forgive so that the matter can be quickly pushed away. The failure to give congregations opportunity to deal with the emotional consequences of betrayal commonly forces those emotions inward into sabotaging or divisive behaviour, frequently resulting in destructive divisions and scape-goating within the community.

Forgiveness is an ethical issue, not just a psychological or theological one. Discerning and acting on what is required for doing justice on behalf of victims in situations of assault and abuse, though often difficult in the immediate situation, is the most faithful response to make. In the long term, it is the best way of laying a foundation for recovery for the victim, the most effective way of preventing further damage within the community, and the most durable way of restoring damage that has been done.

NOTES

1. Standing for "*Sexual Harassment Is Violence; Effective Redress Stops It.*"

2. A method which Beverly Harrison calls a "liberation social ethics methodology" and Katie Cannon calls "emancipatory praxis."

3. *Alive Now*, the U.S. United Methodist Communications publication reprinted it the following year. A number of therapists in Australia and New Zealand have asked permission to photocopy it to give to clients. A church elder in Minnesota asked permission to copy it to distribute through her church and to her Council of Bishops. A social worker working in a prison rehabilitation program, from which church chaplains had been banned because their loving assurances prevented prisoners from accepting responsibility for their actions, asked permission to reproduce and use the paper with the prisoners. I continued to receive letters from around Australia up to five years later from women telling me how much they appreciated the paper and telling me their story of abuse within a church and invariably the failure of church leaders to deal with it effectively.

4. http://www.forgiver.net

5. One of the few who has is Marie Fortune who raises questions about the practice of forgiveness in the context of sexual assault in her two books *Is Nothing Sacred?* and *Sexual Violence: The Unmentionable Sin*. Materials from The Center for the Prevention of Domestic and Sexual Violence consistently address the issue from within an

ethical and justice-making framework. The Center for the Prevention of Sexual and Domestic Violence is an interreligious educational resource located in Seattle, Washington, USA. www.cpsdv.org

6. A good example of this is L. Gregory Jones' text, *Embodying forgiveness.*, Jones, L. G. (1995). *Embodying forgiveness: A theological analysis.* Grand Rapids, William B. Eerdmans.

Jones attempts a detailed evaluation of different perspectives on forgiveness, presenting his own understanding of forgiveness as "not so much a word spoken, an action performed, or a feeling felt as it is an embodied way of life in an ever-deepening friendship with the Triune God and with others" (p.xii). Though he identifies a range of issues involved in thinking about forgiveness, after reading the book it is extremely difficult to remember exactly what has been said or how one would apply it to a situation one encounters. I would argue that this complexity and abstraction, that frequently characterises theological reflection, does not further or clarify understanding, but has contributed to the ambiguity around forgiveness. This creates a practical situation in which those with power impose the understanding and practice that serves their interests.

BIBLIOGRAPHY

Barber, B. (1991). Forgiveness is for the future. In A. Amos (ed.), *Victims into victors: Beyond domestic violence.* Melbourne, Uniting Church Press. Pp. 47-50.

Baumeister, R. F., and J. Juola Exline et al. (1998). The victim role, grudge theory, and two dimensions of forgiveness. In E. J. Worthington (ed.). *Dimensions of forgiveness: Psychological research and theological perspectives.* Philadelphia, Templeton Foundation Press. Pp.79-104.

Blumenthal, D. (1993). *Facing the abusing God: A theology of protest.* Louisville, Westminster: John Knox Press.

Browning, D. S. (1976). *The moral context of pastoral care.* Philadelphia: The Westminster Press.

Comstock, G. (1976). "The role of social and behavioral science in policy-making for television." *Journal of Social Issues* 32(4): 157-76.

Derrida, J. (2001). *On cosmopolitanism and forgiveness.* London, Routledge.

Dowrick, S. (1997). *Forgiveness and other acts of love: Finding true value in your life.* Ringwood: Viking.

Flanigan, B. (1992). *Forgiving the unforgivable: Overcoming the bitter legacy of intimate wounds.* New York: Macmillan.

Herman, J. (1992). *Trauma and recovery.* New York: Basic Books.

Heyward, C. (1987). *Revolutionary forgiveness: Feminist reflections on Nicaragua.* Maryknoll, N.Y.: Orbis.

Horsfield, P. (1994). Forgiveness and reconciliation in situations of sexual assault. Sydney, Commission on Women and Men, Uniting Church in Australia.Occasional Paper.

Jones, L. G. (1995). *Embodying forgiveness: A theological analysis.* Grand Rapids: William B. Eerdmans.

Kairos Theologians, T. (1985). *The Kairos Document, second impression.* Braamfontein.

Kuhn, T. (1970). *The structure of scientific revolutions.* Chicago: University of Chicago Press.

Kurzynski, M. J. (1998). "The virtue of forgiveness as a human resource management strategy." *Journal of Business Ethics* 17(1): 77-85.

Montiel, C. J. (2000). "Constructive and destructive post-conflict forgiveness." *Peace Review* 12(1): 95-101.

Muller-Fahrenholz, G. (1996). *The art of forgiveness: Theological reflections on healing and reconciliation*. Geneva: WCC Publications.

Murphy, J. G., and J. Hampton (1988). *Forgiveness and mercy*. Cambridge: Cambridge University Press.

Oates, J. C. (1996). *We were the Mulvaneys*. London: Fourth Estate.

Russell, L. (1993). *Church in the round: Feminist interpretations of the church*. Louisville, Westminster: John Knox.

Simon, S., and S. Simon (1990). *Forgiveness: How to make peace with your past and get on with your life*. New York: Warner Books.

Stoltenberg, J. (1989). *Refusing to be a man: Essays on sex and justice*. New York, Meridian.

Telfer, W. (1959). *The forgiveness of sins: An essay in the history of Christian doctrine and practice*. London: SCM Press.

Tutu, D. (1999). *No future without forgiveness*. New York: Image Books.

Worthington, E. J., Ed. (1998). *Dimensions of forgiveness: Psychological research and theological perspectives*. Philadelphia: Templeton Foundation Press.

Worthington, E. J. (1998). The pyramid model of forgiveness: Some interdisciplinary speculations about unforgiveness and the promotion of forgiveness. In E. J. Worthington (ed.), *Dimensions of forgiveness: Psychological research and theological perspectives*. Philadelphia: Templeton Foundation Press. Pp. 107-138.

Sexual Abuse, Forgiveness and Justice: A Journey in Faith

James S. Evinger
Dorthea L. Yoder

SUMMARY. The Christian precept of forgiveness is examined in the context of sexual abuse committed against adults and children in Protestant congregations. Two vignettes and accompanying commentary present issues and problems related to an application for reinstatement to office by a minister whose ordination was suspended, and a proposal regarding restitution for victims. A third vignette is an account of an authentic act of forgiveness by a congregation's lay leaders that, as expression of their faith, honors a commitment to make justice for victims. *[Article copies available for a fee from The Haworth Document Delivery Service: 1-800-HAWORTH. E-mail address: <docdelivery@haworthpress.com> Website: <http://www.HaworthPress.com> © 2002 by The Haworth Press, Inc. All rights reserved.]*

KEYWORDS. Child sexual abuse, clergy sexual abuse, clergy sexual misconduct, forgiveness, justice, reinstatement, restitution, sexual exploitation

The religious community must set upon a very difficult journey to expose the disturbing and painful reality that adults and children have been sexually exploited in congregations. This egregious reality must be named for what it

[Haworth co-indexing entry note]: "Sexual Abuse, Forgiveness and Justice: A Journey in Faith." Evinger, James S., and Dorthea L. Yoder. Co-published simultaneously in Journal of Religion & Abuse (The Haworth Pastoral Press, an imprint of The Haworth Press, Inc.) Vol. 4, No. 4, 2002, pp. 71-88; and: *Forgiveness and Abuse: Jewish and Christian Reflections* (ed: Marie M. Fortune, and Joretta L. Marshall) The Haworth Pastoral Press, an imprint of The Haworth Press, Inc., 2002, pp. 71-88. Single or multiple copies of this article are available for a fee from The Haworth Document Delivery Service [1-800-HAWORTH, 9:00 a.m. - 5:00 p.m. (EST). E-mail address: docdelivery@haworthpress.com].

is–sinful, immoral, illegal and unethical behavior that is intolerable. This truth has forced us, the authors, as clergy to reflect on what is at the heart and soul of our own community of faith. The sad reality of sexual exploitation captures the ways our church has failed the victims and protected the perpetrators.

The path to truth leads to questions that press hard and require discernment. One longstanding problem regarding those who sexually abuse others is the Christian precept of forgiveness. How shall we practice forgiveness of those in our midst who so fundamentally violated others? In the face of such a daunting task, it is heartening to remember the insight of a Trappist monk quoted in Wendy M. Wright's *The Vigil*: "To be a Christian does not mean knowing all the answers; to be a Christian means being willing to live in the part of the self where the question is born."[1]

In this essay, we traverse the place where the question of forgiveness is born by presenting three vignettes with commentary. The events we describe are from proceedings related to sexual boundary violations in the Presbyterian Church (U.S.A.), the denomination to which we belong.[2] The conflicting array of rhetoric and images that were invoked in reference to forgiveness forced us to wonder and search. What are the moral and spiritual values that define and motivate behavior in regard to forgiveness? In the current practice of forgiveness in our church, whose needs are actually met? Is forgiveness ever misapplied? What happens in a community when authentic forgiveness is honored? The questions are disruptive, and the search for answers led us to be more honest, resolute and faithful.

The journey to truth recognizes that the precept of forgiveness exists not as an abstract theory, but as a practical component of the religious community and its complex culture that includes: formal role and also personal relationships; linguistic and symbolic systems that convey meaning and beliefs; institutional settings with long histories and elaborate dynamics; disparities based on gender, class and ethnicity. Out of many possibilities, there are four contextual and systemic factors that are essential to this exploration of forgiveness.

The first factor is the nature of the violation. Before the practice of forgiveness is even considered, the nature of the offense that was committed must be clearly identified. Clergy, regardless of whether they acknowledge it, are in a position of unequal power compared to laity. The people for whom they minister are the ones who grant the office and role to clergy as a sacred privilege. It is the people of Jesus Christ who confer as a holy trust the title of clergy upon those who serve in God's name. The people's act of sanctioning their religious leaders precedes the people's act of placing before their religious leaders an invitation to enter their souls. It is this power of trust to engage people in intimate matters of ultimate meaning that is the foundation for the potential to abuse that trust. Any action that betrays, manipulates or coerces others sexually is an unconscionable abuse of that sacred trust. When clergy violate this covenant, they abuse the power of the office and the role.

The second factor is the realization that if the church is to change the way it deals with sexual exploitation and molestation by its leaders, we can no longer be naïve. No longer can we minimize wrongful behaviors by our ignorance of the problems, avoid conflict and disruption by our concealment of those problems under a cloak of secrecy or deny their gravity by relocating the offender. Neither can we be naïve about forgiveness. The safety and health of our communities and the individuals within them is at stake.

The next contextual factor is the nature of ministry as a profession. Clergy as professionals are more than people who respond to a vocational call and receive pay for their work. A profession is based on an evolving body of knowledge and theory generated by its practitioners. A profession functions through a peer review process in which members set standards for education, skill and character; interview and admit applicants; certify those qualified; and, supervise practitioners. Professional competency and integrity in ministerial practice require establishing clear pastoral, emotional, spiritual, psychological and physical boundaries. We need professional codes of ethical conduct that permit no flexibility regarding sexual abuse. Clergy must be held accountable to, at least, the same standards of ethical behavior about sexualized relationships as are professionals who are licensed to establish fiduciary relationships, i.e., nurses, physicians, teachers, lawyers, certified social workers and mental health professionals. We must be clear that forgiveness does not negate accountability to the standards of a religious community, a profession or secular society's criminal and civil statutes.

The final contextual factor is the religious community's responsibility to be vigilant and on constant guard, watching for signs manifested by the sexual predator who uses the privilege and license of ministry as opportunity to hunt and exploit those who are vulnerable. The predator is typically charismatic and ingratiating, able to charm and disarm in order to achieve the exact, desired response. The precise skills used by the predator to groom victims also elicit trust and support from the larger community, creating an aura that makes discovery of perpetration unlikely. There must be effective counterbalances to the offender who isolates and silences his victims through secrecy, dependence or intimidation as part of the pattern of commission. Prevention and intervention measures must include obligatory screening, background checks, mandatory training, mandatory reporting, complaint procedures, intervention strategies and guidelines, victim support measures, discipline policies and mandatory disclosure. A church's well-meaning intention to forgive must never negate the necessity to create a safe environment, especially for people who are spiritually vulnerable. Forgiveness must not be used to betray victims again.

Telling the following events in the form of vignettes was a painful and necessary part of our journey into the discussion of forgiveness. In part a lament, this was an act of faith that led us to the place where the question of forgiveness is born. It is to that center that the people of Jesus Christ are compelled to go after having failed those who trusted that their sisters and brothers would protect them.

I. THEOLOGICAL BAIT AND SWITCH

May 25, 1999
First Presbyterian Church, Albion, NY

The declarative sentence is intoned with understated solemnity. "I know God has forgiven me." It is a self-report with no accompanying verification. Spoken without contrition for the sin or gratitude for the forgiveness, this notice comes as a fleeting reference in a series of justifications. The speaker is John Smith (pseudonym), and he comes before the Presbytery of Genesee Valley, Presbyterian Church (U.S.A.), at its regular business meeting to request that it reinstate him to the office of minister of word and sacrament in our denomination. He lost his standing at an ecclesiastical trial on March 1, 1996, at which time he admitted in a plea of *nolo contendre* to two charges of sexual abuse committed against congregants in the church that he pastored in Oregon in the 1970s. This is his first attempt to gain reinstatement.

Mr. Smith will not explicate the meaning of forgiveness today, either doctrinally or personally. It is sufficient for his purpose simply to invoke the reality of forgiveness in human history, and to name the source as divine. He adds this to the other reasons on his list of why his standing as an ordained minister should be restored.

Claiming forgiveness is a subtle and enticing move. It appeals to our need to offer solace and compassion to one in trouble, and our impulse to welcome the prodigal home. The sentimental logic of his syllogism is that he is entitled to have his ordination back once we forgive him. By this reasoning, the responsibility to offer forgiveness shifts the burden for moral behavior from him to us.[3]

Claiming forgiveness is also a bold move with a distinct edge to it. Who among us would dare to vote against *forgiveness*? Who has the audacity to vote against *God*? We, the progeny of John Calvin and his gloomy sense of the inevitability of sin, are a people whose worship every Sunday morning draws us together in a unison prayer of confession. And then that same worship offers us the assurance of pardon for our sins. Forgiveness is in our liturgical blood and bones.

Mr. Smith would have us substitute a legitimate question about himself and his qualifications for church office with a diversion in the form of a referendum on an essential tenet of our beliefs. The New Testament premise is, indeed, that God forgives sinners, including this one who sexually exploited vulnerable people by misusing the religious office that was conferred upon him in the name of Jesus Christ. He turned his ordination certificate into a hunting license. But forgiveness alone is not sufficient cause to justify conferring the office upon him once more. Forgiveness does not equal reinstatement. He is attempting theological bait and switch. The real question is whether one who previously disqualified himself by his unethical and unprofessional behavior is now fit to hold the same office.

Being forgiven by God is an instrumental act. Forgiveness creates new possibilities for authentic relationships rooted in righteousness that derives from Jesus Christ. God's forgiveness is active and redemptive, never static. It is a gift that always holds a functional promise.[4] It works to transform our state of alienation and moves us into God's *shalom*. It invites us, as individuals and as a community of faith, to relate in new ways toward God, our neighbors and the strangers in our midst. Forgiveness of Mr. Smith's wrongful behavior should be but an antecedent to a new pattern that works for the just benefit of those whom he harmed, rather than to serve him.[5] When he invokes the reality of forgiveness as an absolute, he disconnects it from its instrumental role, strips it from its spiritual purpose and turns it into a legalism. This permits him to conflate forgiveness and ordination. If we extend to him the former, he expects to receive the latter. But his reductionism is wrong. God forgives us all, but not all of us who are forgiven are ordained by the church. If forgiveness equals reinstatement to ordained office, then the outcome would be to maintain the status quo of clergy dominance in the church. The practice of forgiveness, as proposed by Mr. Smith today, is a way to go through the motions of accountability. Forgiveness on his terms is a large broom that sweeps under the carpet the enduring consequences to his victims that resulted when he exploited his ordained authority. His conflation of ordination and forgiveness diminishes both.

Mr. Smith makes other assertions to justify reinstatement to ordained office. He reports that he has been in therapy and spiritual direction since the trial. We are being tempted with another theological bait and switch. Who among his enlightened colleagues would oppose therapy or spiritual direction? His unspoken message is that he has been rehabilitated. His implicit equation is that therapy plus spiritual direction equals change, and change entitles one to reinstatement. He glosses over the fact that these activities were conducted apart from our church and away from our powers of discernment. The therapy was at a secular institution, and the spiritual direction was private through an agency. However commendable these works may be, therapy and spiritual direction do not in themselves ensure that he has altered the behaviors and attitudes that culminated in his misusing his religious identity, professional status and ecclesiastical sanction as means to groom and exploit his victims. As a commentator wryly observed, "Sitting in a church pew on Sunday morning will no more make you a Christian than sitting on tires in your garage will make you a car." Mr. Smith's sophistry insults both the nature and purpose of ordination and of forgiveness. Even if Mr. Smith had produced evidence of therapeutic change, he had to acknowledge or declare responsibility for the harm that he inflicted.

Following his ecclesiastical trial, Mr. Smith was evaluated by a comprehensive assessment program for professionals who used their role to violate fiduciary boundaries. The program was through the psychiatry department of a major New York City academic medical center. However, following treatment, he did not seek a reassessment consistent with the evaluating program's clinical standards. There is no competent third party evaluator to vouch for him. But, even if this perpetrator is now a new man clinically and spiritually, that in itself is not sufficient cause to reinstate him. Ordination to office is not a right of the individual. In our church, ordination is a three-party covenant. It originates with an intentional God who calls a person to service. It continues in the individual who responds affirmatively. The covenant is completed when the community of faith endorses the call and certifies the fitness of the person. Ordination is always a living relationship, never a professional's entitlement. Ordination is a trust conferred by God's people, not a clerical right. When a minister breaks the covenant of ordination, forgiveness does not intrinsically heal that breach and automatically restore the offender to the entrusted office. Mr. Smith's approach may be emotionally compelling, but it is theologically flawed.

His approach is, indeed, emotionally compelling. When Mr. Smith leads us to equate the act of withholding forgiveness from him with the act of withholding his ordination, he appeals to a need to avoid feelings of guilt. Some at this meeting follow his lead and pejoratively label making the decision about reinstatement as judging another. Scripture is cited as prohibiting us from exercising a power that is best left to God: "Judge not, that you be not judged." (Matthew 7:1, NRSV). Others of us display the need to avoid guilt by citing another scripture: "Let anyone among you who is without sin be the first to throw a stone . . . " (John 8:7, NRSV).[6] Suddenly, a credible exercise of accountability has been redefined as an unjust act of hypocrisy. The generalized feeling that we all are sinners is suddenly palpable. This feeling, however inappropriate, has paralyzed those assembled from taking reasonable and responsible measures. "There but for the grace of God go I" is etched in the furrowed brows of some of the gathered faces. Just the prospect of acting to withhold ordination elicits feelings of guilt, and those feelings overwhelm the ability to discern the real issue: is Mr. Smith fit for office now? Some of us rush to sacrifice justice on an altar of forgiveness.

It is a sad commentary that we expend so much attention and time on the offender in contrast to how little we consider his victims. No one asks about those who were hurt by Mr. Smith's actions or what it will take to restore for them the church that he defiled. No one inquires whether clergy as a group need to ask the victims of clergy sexual abuse to forgive our institutional sins over the years when we failed to investigate or hold accountable the predatory clergy in our midst. Like an echo from Ezekiel 34, we did not stop the shepherds who devoured their sheep. We colluded by failure of moral imagination to identify with the victims and by absence of spiritual courage to confront the abusers, but we neither confess nor seek forgiveness for our sins. Our denomination's polity does not even ensure that Mr. Smith's victims have a right to speak to his application for reinstatement. Forgiveness. Dear God, we have so much to learn.

II. WWJWZTD

February 21, 2001
First Presbyterian Church, Victor, NY

The Presbytery of Genesee Valley has convened a special meeting in a nearly 200-year-old church on an upstate New York winter evening. Lay commissioners and clergy have come to vote on whether we will transmit to the denomination's highest legislative body an overture to amend our denomination's constitution. Our numbers are quite small. Given the fierce cold, one must either be very, very loyal to our standing obligation to participate in such deliberations, or else be very, very interested in the single-item agenda. God has been fair tonight; we get a mixture of both types.

The proposed language would amend the "Rules of Discipline" section of our *Book of Order*, the volume that is the polity portion of the Church's constitution. The amendment would permit a Church judicial panel to recommend that the person found guilty of sexual abuse make voluntary restitution to the person who was abused. Note the key words: "permit," "recommend" and "voluntary." However qualified these words are, they nevertheless boldly challenge the norms of our judicial proceedings. Our Church is not ready for the courage of mandatory language that would *require* restitution in such cases.

Consider the present situation. The abuse victim literally has no right to be heard at the trial of her offender except as a witness. If the trial results in a finding of guilt, there is no provision in our judicial rules to ensure that the victim may make a statement to the judicial panel about the impact of the offender's harm on her life, or to entitle the victim to speak for the record about what she believes would make for healing and justice. The New York State criminal code gives a victim more rights in a secular proceeding than our Church does in an ecclesiastical one.

The debate tonight is mercifully conducted without many parliamentary constraints. It ricochets between comments that are wise and those riddled with factual errors. Some statements are substantive, while others focus on the arcane procedures of polity. The preponderance of speakers is male. Too easily, the discussion drifts into abstractions. It soon becomes apparent that only a very small percentage of us are experienced in the intricacies and stresses of an ecclesiastical trial. Over the last 12 years, our presbytery has convened only two trials on charges related to sexual boundary violations committed.

A pastor from a conservative congregation anxiously asserts that the proposed language is punitive, but accurately points out that punishment is contrary to the purpose of discipline as defined by our Church constitution. His indignation taps into a latent reserve of fear about the overture. In our role as proponents, we reply that restitution as a voluntary act is a free choice made by the offender, and therefore is not an imposed punishment per se. We go further. We suggest that restitution will, in fact, be in the offender's best spiritual interests by identifying a clear behavioral outcome of one component of repentance. A few eyebrows arch in recognition of this insight. We cite scriptures that describe how restitution was integral to the legal and moral code of Israel, and point to making amends as part of the 12 steps in Alcoholics Anonymous recovery program.[7] Heads nod in silent assent.

We are using an inductive approach to the debate, and while it deliberately puts us on the defense at the outset, it allows us to scratch where they say they itch. Our responses are educational in content and reassuring in tone. We confidently reply to the critics tense remarks with phrases like, "I'm glad you bring up that important point . . ." This calm strategy allows the opposition to name its resistance and demonstrates that that we recognize their concerns. It de-escalates the tension, and presents us opportunities to address specific worries, all the while offering reasonable explanations. Our credibility grows stronger. The momentum begins to shift to those who support the overture.

A woman from a city church rises to her feet to speak. She dislikes what she has heard because it does not mention love. She condemns our discourse as discordant and disruptive, and proclaims that it sows dissension in the body of Christ. Suddenly, she invokes the question of what Jesus would do, and then supplies her own answer, "WWJD? It's in the Lord's Prayer. He taught us to pray for forgiveness." She abruptly bows her head, and pronounces the familiar words, "Our Father, who art in heaven . . ." People around the room begin to join her, and the rote prayer picks up volume. She is joined by those who respectfully defer to the tradition of offering this prayer in unison, and also by those who do not want to abandon her to a solitary recital. On "Amen," she sits down. The room is very quiet. We've been chastened like children, and coerced by an act that terminated serious discourse and stifled real disagreement. Prayer was used a prooftext, and wielded like a weapon. It is suddenly shameful to do anything less than the Messiah would supposedly do. The silence is awkward.

After the meeting, her pastor privately promises that he will talk to her about Luke 19:1-10. It is the story of Zacchaeus, a chief tax collector who enriched himself at the expense of those he defrauded. When he meets Jesus, he is filled with an inner conviction of sin, and is so truly repentant that he comprehends he must right his wrongs. Authentic repentance compels him to act ethically toward his victims even before Jesus has overtly forgiven him. He does not need to be told what to do. The pastor vows to tell the woman from his congregation about Zacchaeus' promise to make restitution to those whom he had hurt. (Zacchaeus' vow, in fact, is that he will make fourfold restitution.) Her pastor recognizes the simple truth that we mortals, finite and fallible, are not Jesus, and that the real question is not what *Jesus* would do, but what Jesus would prefer that *we* do. The challenge is how we as disciples shall respond to the enduring realities of human sin and human hurt. Our moral imagination is not well-served if we identify with Jesus the Christ and ask what he would do. The better question is, "What would Jesus want Zacchaeus to do?" WWJWZTD?

Our task as people of faith is not to self-impose a Messianic template of perfection and divinity onto the human frame. Jesus had his calling, and we have ours. Our responsibility is to hold offenders within the religious community accountable for their rule violations and relational harms, and to work with victims for what makes for healing and justice.[8] The offender's self-centered expression of guilt must be confronted when presented in such a way that only our offer of forgiveness will redeem him from a debilitating emotional stasis of remorse and pity. Rather, his guilt must be transformed into conscience and responsibility for reparative action that authentically serves the victim. Forgiveness must never be permitted to supplant the necessity that offenders make right what was wronged. Forgiveness that is not predicated ethically on justice for the victim is cheap grace.

Similarly, a religious community's abstract obligation to offer collective absolution must never supplant its responsibility to extend careful, personal acts that will repair the ripped garment of trust that formerly sheltered those who are vulnerable. Reparative actions restore the victim to wholeness and the community to integrity. Neither should forgiveness obviate the community's responsibility to utilize its disciplinary process to validate the truth of the offender's perpetration nor the community's need to attend to harms committed against the victims.[9] Jesus called us to do the hard work that makes for *shalom* in broken lives, including persevering amidst the conflicts and tensions that forgiveness alone does not eliminate. Zaccheaus had it right.

III. IF DISCIPLES WERE SILENT . . .

March 25, 2001
Penfield Presbyterian Church, Penfield, NY

> Lord, hear our words.
> Lord, listen to our hearts.
> We confess that we have turned our heads.
> We have averted our eye.

These words, spoken as prayer, rise before God from the people gathered in a suburban church. The litany of confession is led tonight by an elder, an officer of the congregation. A mother and a highly respected professional in the community, she speaks softly in a resolute, clear voice. The congregation joins and responds antiphonally from adjacent pews.

> We have believed that abuse could not happen here.
> We have denied that it did.

Behind her, six stones are on the communion table at the front of the sanctuary. They were placed carefully in a silent offering by six youth from the congregation. Each stone symbolizes a child or an adolescent who has been identified as a victim of child sexual abuse by a former member of the church. His crimes were committed during the decades that he was a prominent lay leader in the church's extensive youth program and its Boy Scouts troop. He was an adult sanctioned and entrusted to guide children. He was also an ordained deacon who took vows to care in the name of Jesus Christ for those in need. Instead, he used his status in the church and his personal charisma to target victims, groom them and then exploit them sexually during a 20-year period. He was a wolf at the sheepfold in shepherd disguise. The gravity of his behavior is measured by our knowledge that acts against one victim fell within the criminal statute of limitations in New York, and led to his arrest and indictment. Two days before this service, he had pleaded guilty to two criminal counts in that case.[10] Tonight is the first time that the congregation has been informed of the total number of his known victims.

> We hoped someone else would help.
> We thought that someone else would take it away.

After each stone was presented, an adult from the congregation stepped forward, took a piece of cloth and covered it, rendering the stones hidden from our view. The cloths symbolize the lost opportunities to disclose the perpetrator's name and actions to the congregation. It was over four years ago when the two clergy and the elected lay leaders first learned of the molestation from one of his victims. It was two and years eight months after that until the name of the name of the perpetrator would be disclosed to the congregation. The cloths also demonstrate the leader's refusal to face the victims and their families.

> We have looked away . . .
> . . . when we could have looked for a way to comfort.

It is not just members of this congregation who come to this Service of Healing. Sitting in one pew is a man in his early 40's. His parents, who belong to a prominent Methodist congregation, accompany him. Each brings long-standing, private hurts. Several decades before, the pastor of their church had molested the man when he was a young adolescent. He told his parents, and they promptly reported the pastor to the Methodist bishop, but, in an all too frequent scenario that transcends denomination, the bishop only removed the problem from the immediate locale. He transferred the perpetrator to another congregation. At the time, the family was grateful, but the lack of accountability and resolution in that case still haunts them. They heard of this service and are attending because they want to witness a church, any church, confess in public what happened to its children at the hands of a significant religious leader. Any satisfaction for them tonight will be that which comes vicariously, but it will be better than none at all.

> We have covered our ears . . .
> . . . when the truth was painful to hear.

Another elder stands before the congregation. She worked diligently and courageously the last two and a quarter years to move the leadership of her church to disclose the truth of perpetration to the congregation. She formally represented the leadership in the criminal investigation by the New York State Police that led to the arrest, indictment, conviction and imprisonment of the offender. She fought to make visible the needs of the victims. She reads from the third gospel: "And some of the Pharisees in the crowd said to [Jesus], 'Teacher, order your disciples to stop.' He answered, 'I tell you, if these were silent, the stones would shout out.' (Luke 19:39-40, NRSV). She looks at the six stones on the communion table, and then back to the congregation. Her commentary is a single sentence and is spoken with a certainty born deep in faith. "This verse tells us that truth cannot be silenced."

> We have waited . . .
> . . . when we could have acted.

She addresses the father of one of the victims. In 1997, his son was the first to come forward and tell the pastor of this church that the revered youth leader had sexually molested him. The son asked that the truth be told and that other children be made safe from further harm. It not until the pastor had resigned in 1999 and she was assigned responsibility for the case that the church leaders finally began to act in ways that honored the victim's two requests. She speaks directly to the father because she cannot address the son. Within the past year, he died suddenly and prematurely of natural causes. Neither he nor his mother lived to see this service and the full fruits of their labors on behalf of other victims. With the father's permission, she honors the young man by disclosing his name to the congregation for the first time.

> We offer our thanks to you and God for Jeff's bravery. He was the first to come forth and tell the truth. For his faith in God, we give thanks. For helping us to become a better people for Jesus Christ, we give thanks. For his ability to imagine that this healing come occur through this pain, we give thanks. For his resilience in spite of adversity, we give thanks. He knew he was loved and supported by his family, and we thank you for that. Because of the bravery of Jeff and of you, we now have a face to be able to see that this is all real.

> I would like to offer an apology on behalf of the congregation, both to you and to all of the other victims and their families. For those of us that knew and did not speak out, we are sorry. For those of us that asked not to know we are sorry. For those of us that knew and did not fight hard enough for the truth to be told, we are sorry. For taking so long to come to this point, we are sorry. We acknowledge that we all have acted in ways that have disappointed each other and God. For this we seek forgiveness from you and from God.

The silence as she speaks is palpable. In stillness that comes only from a church gathered in worship, quiet tears freely fall on Jeff's father's cheeks. This is a transforming moment. For the first time in over four years, the congregation is guided corporately to reflect on the perpetration in terms of the children. Tonight's consideration of victims leads the congregation to face its culpability.

A genteel, older couple begins to comprehend that by not supporting those who called for a full disclosure when the announcements were first made to the congregation, they indirectly contributed to an environment of denial and avoidance that simultaneously protected a criminal offender and put their own grandchildren at risk.[11] A mother sits between her pre-adolescent daughter and adolescent son whom she intentionally brought to the service because they know the victim in the criminal case. She extends her hands to hold theirs. She offers comfort to her children and seeks to draw solace for herself in return.

Those who remember Jeff growing up as a child in the congregation's programs are in evident distress upon disclosure of his name. After the service, a former officer of the church will recall fond memories of Jeff and his parents. This man was among those who had voted not to know the offender's name when the board was initially informed. He will quote in a shaking voice from the poetry of Emily Dickinson to express his feelings: "Remorse-is Memory-awake/Her parties all astir-/A Presence of Departed Acts-/At window-and at Door-/It's Past-set down before the Soul/And lighted with a match-Perusal-to facilitate-/And help Belief to stretch-"[12]

After the original discovery of child sexual abuse in their church, the leaders defined the issue of forgiveness as a matter of faith. They asked themselves whether they would extend forgiveness to an offender in the congregation. The question, however, was an abstraction because they chose for two and a half years not to know the offender's name. They never engaged in the difficult practice of forgiveness. Their definition of the problem also distanced themselves from facing the risk posed to their church's children by an admitted pedophile. Forgiveness requires hard work, and they shirked it. Tonight's service restates the issue of forgiveness as the leader's culpability in relation to the victims. Under state law, they were the officers of a not-for-profit corporation. By colluding to keep a secret, they failed a fiduciary duty to protect the church's corporate interests by failing to protect the children of the congregation. Forgiveness is still a matter of faith tonight, but now it is the leaders who must seek it.

The leader's act of seeking forgiveness is a victim-oriented hermeneutic that prompts new behavior and so releases new energy into the community. The prior pattern of concealment was a perpetrator-oriented hermeneutic that shut down communication, prevented accountability, devolved to the advantage of the perpetrator and left children exposed to abuse. Telling the truth as part of seeking forgiveness sends the clear message tonight that perpetrators will not be hidden in secrecy, regardless of their role status or personal ties to congregational leaders. Seeking forgiveness is an act that validates victims and helps protect people who are at risk for future harm.[13] That this comes from the lay leadership of the congregation reverses a pattern of dependency upon clergy as autonomous decision-makers, and calls forth the gifts of ministry among the people. As the religious community begins to construct forgiveness in relation to the victim's experience, it acts as a community of faith and discovers that the truth borne by victims is critical to the community's wellness and preservation. Victims have the moral authority to be the conscience of the church, but few congregations see the potential. Victims hold the truth, an immeasurable gift, but few congregations recognize, act to receive or apply it. Tonight, in a western New York suburb, one congregation has begun to practice forgiveness.

In the final analysis, the practice of forgiveness is always an act of faith. The churches' sad, historical failure to respond adequately to sexual exploitation through abuse of trust and power is a failure to live in partnership with God who works in human history to redeem and renew broken lives, and to bless a people who hunger and thirst for love and justice. The faith to confess sin is the courage to follow God's Spirit who supercedes our propensity to compromise God's covenant with us. We have dwelt too long in a Babylonian captivity. We have worshipped broken idols of ignorance, denial, fears and avoidance of conflict.[14] Confession of sin is a profession of faith, an act of hope in the promise that God will lead the exiles home.

The simplicity of forgiveness is elegant because it is a profound manifestation of faith in God. The process of forgiveness originates in our soul, and moves outward with an authentic and full confession that drives us to our knees. Forgiveness requires that the truth be told. Truth identifies who was hurt, what harms were inflicted, who caused the hurt and how it happened.[15] To tell the truth about the offender forces an assessment of culpability and holds that person accountable. The act of telling the truth about culpability is a catalyst for the community to examine its responsibility and complicity. Telling the truth about the harms is a way to alert, educate and help prevent new victimization. To tell the truth about the victims requires identifying ways the community can act to make for healing, offer restitution, promote restoration of those injured and work for justice.

All these simple acts of truth-telling are profound manifestations of faith because they require us to risk the uncertainty of the unknown and trust deeply that God's Spirit works to weave order out of chaos. Risk and trust join as faith to give us the courage to live where the questions are born, the place where God gives waters in the wilderness and rivers in the desert.

NOTES

1. Wendy M. Wright, *The Vigil: Keeping Watch in the Season of Christ's Coming.* Quoted in Rita Collett (Ed.), *The Upper Room Disciplines 2002: A Book of Daily Devotions* (Nashville, TN: Upper Room Books, 2001), p. 78.

2. We were participants in these proceedings through our roles with the Committee on Ministry, Presbytery of Genesee Valley, Rochester, N.Y., which exercises oversight of ministers and congregations. Our degree of direct involvement varied, depending on our respective roles.

3. See Ron O'Grady, *The Hidden Shame of the Church: Sexual Abuse of Children and the Church* (Geneva, Switzerland: WCC Publications, 2001), 33: "The pressure on Christians to "forgive and forget"is quite common, but in practice it will often end up as a form of blackmail. It is especially insensitive to those who have been abused . . . now they are being coerced to show forgiveness to the abuser. . . . But if the victims decline to show forgiveness in these circumstances, they will be made to carry an additional sense of guilt in the eyes of the church. They will be seen as bad Christians because they couldn't forgive as they were commanded to do by Christ."See also Catherine J. Foote, *Survivor Prayers: Talking with God about Childhood Sexual Abuse* (Louisville, KY: Westminster/John Knox Press, 1994), 65-66.

4. There is a hopeful, creative, and future-oriented dimension to God's forgiveness. See Dietrich Bonhoeffer, *Creation and Fall* (New York: The Macmillan Co., 1960), 52: "Grace is that which supports [us] over the abyss of nonbeing, nonliving, that which is not created."

5. Our church promotes the resolution of conflict in the name of reconciliation between two parties in tension, and forgiveness is a way to advance reconciliation. However, if the form of that reconciliation does not address the injustice done to the party that was harmed, any so-called resolution will teeter on a false foundation. Forgiveness as a sentimental harmonizing of conflict is a superficial act that perpetuates the original unjust conditions. The ethical implications of forgiveness are expressed theologically by Charles C. West, *The Power to Be Human: Toward a Secular Theology* (New York: Macmillan, 1971), 233: "God in Christ reconciles the world to [God's self] not by compromising with injustice, but by subjecting the world's power to [God's self] and by transforming the unjust [person] through the forgiveness of [one's] sins . . . It breaks through the awful logic of human power–the endless chain of wrong, retribution, and new wrong–and transmutes it, despite itself, into the service of [people]." Forgiveness that does not integrate a transformation of the original unjust relationship contradicts authentic reconciliation.

The Hebrew and New Testament scriptures consistently reveal that God rejects the subversion of religious acts for personal gain. See, for example, Isaiah 58:3-11. The biblical call is for religious acts that benefit those who suffer and are afflicted.

For a contemporary application of this, see L. Gregory Jones, "Tough Love for Sexual Abusers" *Christian Century,* 119(Apr. 24-May 1, 2002), 40: ". . . while Christ's death and resurrection offer us forgiveness, the only way we can appropriately receive that forgiveness is by undertaking repentance. We learn the true liberation of forgiveness when we commit ourselves not to replicate the past but to live into a different future. This repentance also leads us to turn to our own victims and to live in solidarity with victimized people everywhere."

6. A year after these comments were made in a public meeting, a nationally-prominent author noted how these same two scriptures are cited in ecclesiastical situations to

silence debate on the immoral behavior of clergy. See William H. Willimon, *Calling and Character: Virtues of the Ordained Life* (Nashville, TN: Abingdon Press, 2000), 72. He notes that even though the passages are sentimentalized, universalized and taken out of context, they effectively inhibit the appropriate exercise of accountability.

7. See Steps 8 and 9. Alcoholics Anonymous World Services, Inc. (n.d.). The Twelve Steps of Alcoholics Anonymous. Retrieved April 23, 2002, from http://www.alcoholics-anonymous.org/english/E_FactFile/M-24_d6

8. It was beyond our scope to present a definition of justice or systematically explore it as a concept. Our concern is how the Christian church applies forgiveness in the context of sexual boundary violations, and the ways that justice is connected to, or disconnected from, that application. Our thinking is informed by the elements of justice-making identified in Marie M. Fortune et al., *Workshop Manual–Clergy Misconduct: Sexual Abuse in the Ministerial Relationship* (Seattle, WA: Center for the Prevention of Sexual and Domestic Violence, 1992, 1997).

9. For a full articulation of this position, see Carolyn Holderreard Heggen's "Religious Beliefs and Abuse," Chapter 3 in Catherine Clark Kroeger and James R. Beck (Eds.), *Women, Abuse, and the Bible: How Scripture Can be Used to Hurt or Heal* (Grand Rapids, MI: Baker Books, 1996), 26-27: ". . . a facile, quick forgiveness that doesn't appropriately hold the perpetrator of abuse responsible for his behavior not only puts others in danger of his ongoing violence, it likewise decreases the likelihood that he will honestly face his sinful behavior, repent, and get the help he needs to understand and change his destructive patterns of behavior. Pushing for quick forgiveness and cheap mercy not only trivializes the victim's depth of pain and woundedness, but may also rob the perpetrator of the opportunity to experience true repentance and redemption."

See also Catherine J. Foote, *Survivor Prayers: Talking with God about Childhood Sexual Abuse* (Louisville, KY: Westminster/John Knox Press, 1994), 67: "To offer "forgiveness"before the pain has been articulated, the damage assessed, and the work of repentance completed is not the way to recovery. It does not clarify the injustice and it does not heal."

For support of restitution from an evangelical point of view, see Kenneth S. Kantzer, "The Road to Restoration: How Should the Church Treat Its Fallen Leaders?" *Christianity Today,* 31(Nov. 20, 1987):19-22. For an analysis by a proponent of the concept of restorative justice, see Howard Zehr's "Restoring Justice," Chapter 8 in Lisa Barnes Lampman (Ed.), *God and the Victim: Theological Reflections on Evil, Victimization, Justice, and Forgiveness* (Grand Rapids, MI: Eerdmans, 1999), 145: "Crime victims also want restitution. In part this means payment for losses, but more important is the symbolic statement involved. Restitution . . . states implicitly that someone else-not the victim-is responsible. It is a way of denouncing the wrong, absolving the victim, and saying who is responsible . . . Restitution helps with the need for validation *and* vindication . . ."

An application of the concept of restorative justice to a specific context is Desmond Mpilo Tutu's *No Future Without Forgiveness* (New York: Doubleday, 1999). Tutu was appointed by Nelson Mandela, democratically elected president of South Africa, to chair the nation's Truth and Reconciliation Commission that was created after apartheid was dismantled. See especially Chapter 4, "What About Justice?" 49-65. Tutu describes forgiveness as one component of "the healing of breaches, the redressing of imbalances, the restoration of broken relationships . . ."

10. The perpetrator's acts against five of the six victims are now beyond the criminal statute of limitations in New York. However, one set of behaviors did qualify. This case was opened when a minor reported him to the Bureau of Criminal Investigation, New York State Police, in the fall of 1999. After a formal investigation, the offender was arrested on 01/14/00. On 06/02/00, he was indicted by a Monroe County criminal grand jury on one count of sodomy in the second degree, and one count of endangering the welfare of a minor. His attorney moved to suppress his confession to the New York State Police, but the judge ruled on 02/00/01 to deny the motion on the grounds that his testimony that his rights were violated was not credible. On 03/23/01, he pleaded guilty to both counts as indicted, and began serving a jail sentence on 05/18/01. In a related hearing to determine his level of risk assessment under the New York State Sex Offender Registration Act, the judge ruled on 07/27/01 that he be assigned level 3, the highest risk category according to the law. Level 3 requires lifetime registration with legal authorities.

11. Deborah Pope-Lance of Sudbury, MA, consults with congregations and governing bodies on *afterpastor* or *after betrayal ministry*, which she defines as "Any ministry where a previous religious leader engaged in unethical conduct, engaged in sexual misconduct by sexual exploitation, harassment or abuse, sexualized ministerial relationships, abused power or authority, betrayed trust, or violated pastoral role responsibilities." (Workshop handout. Deborah J. Pope-Lance ©1998). She describes five models for understanding afterpastor ministry: conflict resolution; systems theory; justice making/ethics; grief and loss; trauma. Each model has a different basis for framing the nature of the misconduct and its aftermath. Each model applies a specific strategic response that derives from that understanding, and each one has unique strengths and weaknesses. Of the five, the one that most explicitly addresses the circumstances and experiences of the victim(s) is justice making/ethics, a model that draws from the writings and work of Marie M. Fortune. In the other four models, the needs of the victim(s) are secondary to an emphasis on those of the congregation. We report this not to critique either the models or the important and constructive work of Ms. Pope-Lance, but to note the religious community's collective de-emphasis of victims, even after the reality of victimization has been discovered.

12. R.W. Franklin (Ed.), *The Poems of Emily Dickinson (Cambridge, MA: Belknap Press of Harvard University Press, 1999)* 348-349.

13. An interesting discussion of the broader implications of forgiveness and justice for the religious community is developed by Joretta L. Marshall, "Communal Dimensions of Forgiveness: Learning from the Life and Death of Matthew Shepard" *Journal of Pastoral Theology,* (1999), 49-61. She calls for moving beyond personal hurt and pain to consider communal wounding and accountability. Her thesis is "that forgiveness can only be realized when the community of faith struggles with, acknowledges its participation in, and ultimately changes its behavior in respect to injustices experienced by [victims] and their loved ones. Authentic forgiveness joins God's liberative activity as individuals and communities acknowledge and address the multiple layers of hurt and pain experienced as a result of an injustice, changing their actions in response." Forgiveness has a subversive dimension, she continues, in that it "overturns the dynamics of power" and "the culturally normative ways of responding to injustice" to "eventuate in freeing energies toward the development of just relationships."

14. For example, within a local church, the desire to believe that the respected and revered leader could not have committed sexual abuse can be incredibly strong. The possibility of admitting this reality evokes the fear that the church's identity as special and

significant would be destroyed. In one large, Midwestern congregation of middle class, educated professionals, devoted followers of a Protestant clergyman rallied to his defense even after 12 victims came forward to report his offenses. Rather than believe the truth about him, the victims were hatefully described as weak, devious, ensaring and women "who asked for it." The revictimization of the 12 by members of the church was devastating. The option of disbelieving and discrediting the victims was less threatening to the church than the choice of giving up the illusion of the minister, and by extension, the identity of the church, as special. This need for denial not only prevented the healing of the victims, but also averted the congregation's own healing.

15. Abuse, by definition, entails injury or harm. In the context of sexual abuse accomplished through misuse of religious authority, abuse may be experienced in the following domains: physical, especially if the perpetration was accomplished through force; familial, e.g., the enduring effects disrupt or destroy primary relationships; economic, e.g., counseling expenses, or time lost from employment while coping with the effects; religious, e.g., impairing the victim's capacity to participate in a congregation; spiritual, e.g., impairing the victim's ability to trust God or practice a faith; psychological, e.g., introjecting blame for the perpetration against one's self in the form of inappropriate guilt or self-loathing, or symptoms of traumatic stress disorder.

Three Spirits:
One Parish
A Short Story in Four Parts

Marilyn Born

THE SPIRIT OF ALICE:
UNWHOLLY AND UNSEEN

In her short life Alice has walked down the street with a feeling of shame she calls in her head, "Stinky." Most of the time Alice sets the feeling far enough back in her mind to carry on. She bolsters herself by holding her head high and avoiding people's eyes. Quite a few dismiss her as haughty and aloof. Sometimes the fear that "Stinky" shows is overwhelming. Alice retraces her steps, returns home, locks herself in her room and replans her day: sitting on the floor of the shower with her head in her hands until the hot water runs out, reading book after book, talking to a school friend on the phone or sleeping for hours in the middle of the day. On these days some small valued thing goes missing from her brother Jude's room never to be seen again. Except once when an Australian Open finals ticket was unearthed by her father from a metre high pile of clothes and books and junk in Alice's wardrobe. Alice stood by the unearthing, arms

---

[Haworth co-indexing entry note]: "Three Spirits: One Parish. A Short Story in Four Parts." Born, Marilyn. Co-published simultaneously in Journal of Religion & Abuse (The Haworth Pastoral Press, an imprint of The Haworth Press, Inc.) Vol. 4, No. 4, 2002, pp. 89-93; and: *Forgiveness and Abuse: Jewish and Christian Reflections* (ed: Marie M. Fortune, and Joretta L. Marshall) The Haworth Pastoral Press, an imprint of The Haworth Press, Inc., 2002, pp. 89-93. Single or multiple copies of this article are available for a fee from The Haworth Document Delivery Service [1-800-HAWORTH, 9:00 a.m. - 5:00 p.m. (EST). E-mail address: docdelivery@haworthpress.com].

crossed, not sorry all Jude's other things were well and truly gone to the pawn shop.

No one can remember exactly when Alice stopped tidying her room, although family lore claims the phenomenon was sudden. Her mother, Georgina, insisted Alice clear a path from the door to her bed so she could kiss Alice goodnight without fear of stumbling on anything. The cleared path to the bed and a sparkling clean goldfish bowl from which one views pellucid Matilda wandering through weed and grotto are the only things maintained against the mess. And when Matilda jumps out on to the littered floor about once a year, miraculously Alice is there to see this happen or just returned in time to save her. Alice is discerning and magical in her messy room and nothing in her care suffers by foul means.

Georgina is at pains to understand how she created her changeling child, at once angry, fractious, sensitive, charming, indifferent, withdrawn. Jude thinks she is envious of boys and calls her "Jealous Alice." Her father says she is hypersensitive, an artist in the making. Her uncle, who has two daughters, says girls are moody by nature. Her teachers believe, although uneven in her work, Alice will come through as she is very bright. Father James suspects she may be spoilt coming from one of the better off families in the parish.

THE SPIRIT OF FATHER JAMES: UNKNOWING AND UNREPENTANT

In all his parishes Father James has walked down the streets. Children call to him, shop keepers wave and he stops to chat. He has taken for granted his status in the town, the myriad ways he is recognised, respected. He feels grateful for the privilege of being present with parishioners at the most joyful and most painful times of their lives. He feels a great sense of satisfaction in helping others.

On the other hand, Father James has had his fair share of difficulties in parish life. Sometimes trivial disagreements turn into major conflicts and he resents the time wasted putting out the fires. His theological views have come under scrutiny now and again like the time the bishop rapped his knuckles over a homily on the virgin birth. More than once he has questioned his calling: the long hours, the paucity of opportunities and time to socialise outside the parish and keeping up on his reading are definite minuses.

Nothing, however, has prepared Father James for the slump in his self-esteem since the media revelations about *the crisis*, about *the exposure of the dark side of the church*, about the sexual abuse *incidents*, about the *other matter of the cover-ups*.

Walking down the street is not so pleasant these days. If the green grocer doesn't wave, James wonders if he hasn't been seen or whether grocer, Dave, suspects he may be a paedophile too. When the Glucksen girls come running to hold his hand so they can jump from one concrete slab to another without touching the cracks James looks around to see who's watching. And the other day Cathy Bloomsdale laughed when he left his office door ajar! "Doesn't she know what we priests are going through?"

Father James went to seminary with Father Gregory and "didn't suspect a thing." There were half-hearted jokes and rumours and Greg's parish appointments were noticeably short but it didn't enter James's head "that it could have been that!" Father James didn't have time to keep up on every issue. "I'm not the morals police for God's sake." "I can't believe I said that," said Father James.

Father James knows he has to re-educate himself and think about the victim's perspective and their suffering. He knows the feminists have a point about patriarchal power. He knows that! So his raw emotions are reserved for "the sensational media." And Father James can not understand why the public apologies and work on new complaints processes are not received as acts of good faith. Why are those victim support groups never satisfied?? Hasn't anyone heard of forgiveness these days?? Of course! Healing is the next step. I must make a point of this next Sunday and include a prayer about the victim's pain–a long one, decides Father James.

Father James wakes in a sweat on Saturday night. His first thought: "I just want it to be back the way it was."

THE SPIRIT OF CATHY BLOOMSDALE: UNFORGIVING

All her life Cathy has walked along the streets of her neighbourhood. She was a dedicated parish volunteer when she wasn't raising children or relief teaching at local schools. Some found her parish initiatives rather radical and her manner was at times not to the liking of everyone. However, Cathy enjoyed the respect of all. That is until the week about a decade ago when a fellow teacher told Cathy that she suspected Father Greg was interfering with Bryan Smallbone. Cathy Bloomsdale reported Father Gregory in the days before it was mandatory to do so. Cathy had read all the material she had gathered for Father James to read and went to seminars on Violence Against Women and Children in Church Communities. Father James was too shocked to be much help to Cathy the week that changed her life. He was counselling Father Gregory. Cathy explained to Father James why it was not a good idea to go to the court with Father Gregory but couldn't convince him to attend with Bryan and his family instead. She remembers his words to this day: "I just can't see fit to do it Cathy. Greg is a friend and colleague." Cathy picked up her preschooler, Sophie, and took herself to court to sit with Bryan's family.

Walking down the street is not what it was in the beginning. Cathy feels *unclean*. Some of the congregation have avoided her outright. Most are decidedly uncomfortable when they run across her. Lately, though, an old congregant whispered, "I've been meaning to tell you, you did the right thing in the Bryan Smallbone Case." Cathy says thank you and reminds her that it is the "Father Gregory" Case.

Bryan Smallbone and his family moved after the court case. Bryan is doing well compared to the other victims of Father Gregory. Unfortunately they did not have the support needed to come forward as children.

Cathy has moved her voluntary commitment to a secular advocacy group for victim/survivors of clergy violence. She was interviewed on SBS recently and had this to say: "This talk of a resurrection of trust is premature. We haven't witnessed a credible death. The hierarchies of the churches have squandered their opportunities to get it right. It's now up to ordinary Christians. We cannot sit with our shock and grief through another church sponsored round of partial solutions. If we can't demand that church leaders report child abuse what is our faith worth? Jesus was unforgiving on the welfare of a child, 'If anyone causes one of these little ones to stumble.' Sign the petition to the PM demanding an independent inquiry and withhold your tithe until we see real results!"

THE SPIRIT OF ALICE:
SHALL REMAIN DIVISIBLE YET NOT INVISIBLE

Alice struggles to grow older as best she can. She is troubled by awful feelings for herself and others and a dreary outlook she wants to go away. Alice decides: "I need someone to talk to, not just anyone but someone I can trust."

Alice begins to tell Father James' successor, a young charismatic priest fresh from seminary with prizes in theology and social justice, about her childhood. Her tears flood her face and numb her mind for the first time in front of someone else. Her *counsellor* responds by *comforting* her with sex. Alice doesn't feel exactly comforted. Some parishioners become aware of the nature of the pastoral care Alice is receiving. When confronted, their priest vociferously declares his love for Alice and directly leaves the parish and his vocation to marry Alice, who feels at sea more than ever and now loyalty bound. The parish is quietly proud that *these things* can be handled *quietly*. However the marriage relationship sours and on her 23rd birthday, Alice quietly takes her own life, leaving a note giving Matilda to Sophie Bloomsdale (who has a big tank).

Alice's uncle takes the news of his niece's death rather hard, stepping backwards into an elevator shaft on the 16th floor of the building he is constructing. The parish, fond of Alice and not of her uncle, spend their grief at her funeral rather than his.

Alice's priest-come-husband begins *a new life* as a psychotherapist. On certain occasions the spirit of serendipity appears as a bee on the wall of his therapy room and buzzes incessantly around a client until she leaves, often for good.

Georgina lives with her grief and the feelings of not knowing until one day Cathy and Sophie befriend her. Her inertia recedes. Her awareness begins. Never again will she avert her eyes, deafen her ears or hold the naming in. She knows how to pay attention now. Her discernment grows around many things. Her humour returns. All this with her friendships make her strong and away she goes, living in real time, without abstraction, sowing new seeds, administering bitter herbs, finding lost treasure.

First a son-in-law is chewed out rather well and a letter is written to the therapist's board. Then Georgina leaves her husband (who doesn't want to know) and she and Jude slip into the cemetery one moonlit night and remove the words "good and faithful brother" from her brother-in-law's headstone. They replace them with a more fitting epithet. The word spreads. Perception grows in the parish. No charges are laid. The two nieces (and their mother) are invited to tea, often. Their mother often declines. She knows the truth yet keeps it close so remains unassured of freedom. Meanwhile there isn't a day too short for Georgina and Jude to cherish a memory of Alice, to forgive and feel forgiven.

Some time later we find rare friendships have thrived among young Sophie, Jude and the two nieces, Audrey and Beatrice. Fullness of spirit, discernment and active engagement in their world mark them out. The foursome are planning "A Day of Shame and A Month of Withholding Your Giving" around the country until religious leaders put forward effective prevention for clergy violence and professional misconduct.

One summer Sunday, family and friends (excepting as is their custom, clerics) gather for a picnic in Cathy and Georgina's garden. Audrey and Berty spot the new bush right away. Taken, they fetch the "Rose Bible" from the potting shed shelf. They read aloud from the entry thus: "Alice"–small yellow buds, the hue and sheen (indeed aura!) of silkworm cocoons; a most pleasing fragrance; my favourite yellow . . ." Someone says, "Amen."

For Christine and Stephanie

Forgiveness, Reconciliation, and Healing

Catherine T. Coyle

SUMMARY. This article explores two questions: "Are forgiveness and reconciliation synonymous?" and "Are both forgiveness and reconciliation necessary for psychological healing?" The questions are discussed in the context of abuse. A process model of forgiveness is described and relevant research is summarized. The author concludes that forgiveness and reconciliation are not synonymous and, therefore, abuse victims may benefit from choosing to forgive even without reconciling with their abusers. *[Article copies available for a fee from The Haworth Document Delivery Service: 1-800-HAWORTH. E-mail address: <docdelivery@haworthpress.com> Website: <http://www.HaworthPress.com> © 2002 by The Haworth Press, Inc. All rights reserved.]*

KEYWORDS. Forgiveness, reconciliation, abuse

Both forgiveness and reconciliation may be thought of as paths to healing. However, one might reasonably ask whether forgiveness and reconciliation are synonymous as well as whether both are necessary in order for healing to occur following an injury. This paper will explore those questions particularly in the context of abuse.

[Haworth co-indexing entry note]: "Foregiveness, Reconiliation, and Healing." Coyle, Catherine T. Co-published simultaneously in Journal of Religion & Abuse (The Haworth Pastoral Press, an imprint of The Haworth Press, Inc.) Vol. 4, No. 4, 2002, pp. 95-105; and: *Forgiveness and Abuse: Jewish and Christian Reflections* (ed: Marie M. Fortune, and Joretta L. Marshall) The Haworth Pastoral Press, an imprint of The Haworth Press, Inc., 2002, pp. 95-105. Single or multiple copies of this article are available for a fee from The Haworth Document Delivery Service [1-800-HAWORTH, 9:00 a.m. - 5:00 p.m. (EST). E-mail address: docdelivery@haworthpress.com].

ARE FORGIVENESS AND RECONCILIATION SYNONYMOUS?

In attempting to answer this question, it may be useful to define the terms "forgiveness" and "reconciliation." Borrowing from philosopher Joanna North (1987), Enright and the Human Development Study Group (1996, 108) have defined genuine forgiveness as "a willingness to abandon one's right to resentment, condemnation, and subtle revenge toward an offender who acts unjustly, while fostering the undeserved qualities of compassion, generosity, and even love toward him or her." The injured person chooses to give up resentment and retaliation and, instead, offers the undeserved gift of mercy to the wrongdoer. There are a number of noteworthy implications in this definition. First, it is implied that the one who has been injured is aware of the injury and of the unjust nature of the injury. Without such recognition, there would be no need to consider forgiveness. Second, the injured person willingly chooses to forgive and to offer mercy to an undeserving offender. There is no coercion involved in the decision to forgive. Third, the act of forgiveness is the inner response of one individual to another.

The proposed definition of forgiveness does not in any way imply that the perpetrator is not guilty. If there were no guilt on the offender's part, there would be nothing to forgive. Differentiating forgiveness from other possible responses to an unjust injury may provide further clarification. Forgiveness is not pardoning. Pardoning suggests that the offender is spared legal consequences for his/her offense. In the case of abuse, a victim may choose to forgive his/her abuser yet still allow legal penalties to be enforced. Neither is forgiveness condoning (Kolnai, 1973-1974) or excusing (Veenstra, 1992). Both condoning and excusing imply innocence on the offender's part and so forgiveness becomes a moot point. If an abuse victim believes that his/her abuser was not responsible for the abuse, then there is really nothing to forgive. Forgiveness is also not the same as forgetting or denying. Each of these responses may prevent the process of forgiveness from occurring. As Lewis Smedes (1984, 60) has observed, "forgetting may be a dangerous way to escape the inner surgery of the heart that we call forgiving." Likewise, denial may be employed to avoid facing the pain of a very real injury. Taken to the extreme, denial may be evidenced as a reaction formation whereby the abused person believes he/she has forgiven when in fact his/her pain and anger have not been consciously recognized (Hunter, 1978).

Within the proposed question, the second term needing clarification is "reconciliation." The root word, "reconcile," has been defined in *Webster's Dictionary of the English Language* as, "to make friendly again, as after a quarrel," or "to cause to accept something not desired" (1983, 757). Two possible implications follow from Webster's definition. Either the injured and the offender come together again in the spirit of friendship (which suggests interaction of a social sort between them) or the injured person comes to accept something undesirable from the offender. In either case, there is an implied coming together of the two individuals. Enright (2001, 31) defined reconciliation as "the act of two people coming together following separation," again suggesting a physical and behavioral interaction.

In sum then, forgiveness and reconciliation are not the same. Rather, they are two distinct concepts. Forgiveness is an internal response of one individual to another while reconciliation implies that two people, both the injured and the offender, choose to engage in some sort of relationship. This further suggests that both the victim and the abuser willingly choose to make their relationship desirable for both parties. As victims of abuse and those who counsel them well know, abusers are not always willing to change their behavior in order to build desirable relationships with those they have harmed.

ARE FORGIVENESS AND RECONCILIATION BOTH NECESSARY FOR HEALING?

Let us first consider that forgiveness and reconciliation are, in fact, both necessary for healing. If so, then we must logically conclude that an abuse victim who chooses to forgive must also choose to meet the abuser in the spirit of friendship or to at least engage in some form of behavioral interaction. Surely this may be possible and may even represent an ideal outcome following abuse. However, there are numerous circumstances in which this is difficult to imagine.

For example, if the victim has forgiven an abusive parent who happens to be deceased, then obviously there can be no reconciliation for that implies a behavioral coming together. In another case, an abuse victim may offer forgiveness to a perpetrator while the perpetrator refuses to acknowledge any wrongdoing. In such a case, the offer of forgiveness may actually arouse anger and indignation in the perpetrator rather than a spirit of friendship. In still another case, the abused may offer forgiveness, attempt to reconcile, but then suffer further abuse by reentering a dangerous relationship.

An abused person who believes that forgiveness and reconciliation must occur together may arrive at two very different conclusions from the previous examples. On the one hand, the abused may conclude that he/she has not truly forgiven if reconciliation does not also occur. If the abused questions his/her ability or sincerity in terms of forgiveness, he/she may suffer self-condemnation in addition to the very real damage done by the offender. On the other hand, an abuse victim may hesitate to forgive in order to avoid a perceived need to reconcile. If an abused person fears reconciliation, he/she may avoid the issue of forgiveness altogether and bypass an opportunity for healing.

Similarly, clinicians who believe that forgiveness and reconciliation are both required for healing would be hard-pressed to recommend such a dangerous notion as forgiveness. After all, a therapist cannot ethically encourage clients to put themselves in danger. They may even tend to agree with Haber (1991) who has argued that resentment is to be encouraged in the abused as it fosters a sense of self-respect. Forgiveness, according to Haber, demonstrates weakness and a low opinion of the self. This line of reasoning may cause clinicians to view forgiveness as a dangerous path leading to further victimization of their clients.

Let us now consider the implications of the contrary view, that is, that forgiveness and reconciliation are *not* both required for healing. This distinction has very practical consequences when it is clearly understood by both therapist and client that forgiveness of an abuser does not require reconciliation and the possibility of more abuse. Therapists who accept such a distinction are much more likely to encourage and support a client's efforts to forgive an abusive parent or spouse. Also, clients may be more receptive to the possibility of forgiveness and relieved of a good deal of anxiety knowing that the decision to forgive does not put them at further risk.

This view, that forgiveness may bring healing even without reconciliation, has been documented by both empirical research and clinical observations. Therapists and clients who choose to pursue forgiveness may profit from utilizing an empirically tested model of interpersonal forgiveness developed by Enright et al. (1996). Clinical reports also may be useful and suggest that forgiveness, even without reconciliation, offers psychological benefits.

A PSYCHOLOGICAL PROCESS MODEL OF FORGIVENESS

The model described by Enright et al. (1996) consists of twenty units (see Table 1) that describe the path taken when one person forgives another. Note that reconciliation is *not* one of those units. Reconciliation is differentiated from forgiveness, as it is believed to be dependent on the trustworthiness of the offender rather than on the injured person's decision to forgive.

The twenty units of the process model are further divided into four phases: the uncovering, decision, work, and outcome phase. During the uncovering phase, the injured person explores both the effects of the abuse on him/herself as well as his/her response to the abuse. Defense mechanisms that have been used to protect the self from pain are examined (unit 1). If an abused person is employing the defense mechanism of denial, then the process cannot com-

TABLE 1. Processes of Interpersonal Forgiveness

Uncovering Phase

1. Examination of psychological defenses (Kiel, 1986).

2. Confrontation of anger; the point is to release, not harbor, the anger (Trainer, 1981).

3 Admittance of shame, when this is appropriate (Patton, 1985).

4. Awareness of cathexis (Droll, 1984).

5. Awareness of cognitive rehearsal of the offense (Droll, 1984).

6. Insight that the injured party may be comparing self with the injurer (Kiel, 1986).

7. Realization that oneself may be permanently and adversely changed by the injury (Close, 1970).

8. Insight into a possibly altered "just world" view (Flanigan, 1987).

Decision Phase

9. A change of heart, conversion, new insights that old resolution strategies are not working (North, 1987).

10. Willingness to consider forgiveness as an option.

11. Commitment to forgive the offender (Neblet, 1974).

Work Phase

12. Reframing, through role-taking, who the wrongdoer is by viewing him or her in context (Smith, 1981).

13. Empathy toward the offender (Cunningham, 1985).

14. Compassion toward the offender (Droll, 1984).

15. Acceptance, absorption of the pain (Bergin, 1988).

Outcome or Deepening Phase

16. Finding meaning for self and others in the suffering and in the forgiveness process (Frankl, 1959).

17. Realization that self has needed others' forgiveness in the past (Cunningham, 1985).

18. Insight that one is not alone (universality, support).

19. Realization that self may have a new purpose in life because of the injury.

20. Awareness of decreased negative affect and, perhaps, increased positive affect, if this begins to emerge, toward the injurer; awareness of internal emotional release (Smedes, 1984).

Note. This table is an extrapolation from and extension of Enright and the Human Development Study Group (1991). The references at the end of each unit are prototypical examples or discussions of that unit.

mence, as there is no perceived need to forgive. Other likely defense mechanisms include repression and/or withdrawal. With gentle guidance from a sensitive counselor, the abused may become more aware of how he/she has attempted to avoid or cope with the injury. Together, client and therapist also may explore the abused person's experience of anger (unit 2). While anger is a normal, even healthy response following abuse, it can be exhausting over a long period of time. Still another risk of intense and prolonged anger is that it may be displaced onto innocent others. The abused may discover that he/she also feels shame (unit 3) particularly if the abuse has led to some form of humiliation. It is essential that the abused client be assured that he/she is not the guilty party. Rather, it is the abuser who should feel shame. Nonetheless, the abuse victim must have the opportunity to express his/her shame whether it is perceived as valid or not by the therapist. As these responses to abuse are explored, the abuse victim becomes increasingly aware of the amount of energy that has been spent (unit 4) and of the tendency toward cognitive rehearsal of the hurtful event (unit 5). Cognitive rehearsal refers to the replay of the abuse over and over in one's mind. This, too, can deplete the victim's energy and even make it impossible to concentrate on daily activities. The abused may find that he/she frequently compares his/her state with that of the abuser (unit 6) and conclude that he/she has been permanently changed by the injury (unit 7). Meanwhile, the abuser may seem to be free of remorse or pain. Such a comparison may lead to an alteration in the abuse victim's view of justice or fairness (unit 8). As a result, the victim may question whether life is fair and/or whether anyone else shares a similar view of justice. Throughout this uncovering phase, it is useful for the counselor to assure the victim that his/her responses are normal but not necessarily productive over time.

Units 9, 10, and 11 comprise the decision phase of the forgiveness process. As awareness increases and painful emotions surface, the abuse victim may come to the realization that some sort of resolution is necessary (unit 9). At this point, he/she becomes willing to at least explore the possibility of forgiveness (unit 10) and may commit to forgiving the offender (unit 11). Prior to making such a commitment, victims of abuse may need reassurance that forgiveness does not require risky interaction between themselves and their abusers. Abuse victims also may find it easier to decide to forgive if they have received an apology or, at least, some recognition of wrongdoing on the part of their abusers. Unfortunately, both may be unlikely or long in coming. Clinicians must be sensitive to the client's point of progress in order to facilitate this phase. Patience, on the part of both therapist and client, is also essential. The forgiveness journey is a difficult one and victims may need to express and process their anger on more than one occasion as they travel. Even so, a critical point is reached when the abuse victim commits to working toward forgiveness of his/her abuser. It is at this point that the abused person chooses not just to forgive but also to become a *survivor* rather than a victim. In this phase, the survivor's decision imparts a new sense of control; that is in terms of *how* he/she will respond now as well as how he/she will be affected in the future.

Following the critical decision to forgive, the abuse survivor moves into the working phase of the forgiveness process. This phase requires that he/she engage in reframing or enlarging the context in which the offender is viewed (unit 12). The singular purpose of reframing is not to excuse the abusive offender but rather to better understand the offender's behavior. This distinction is significant especially with those who have been abused. By no means should abused persons be led to believe that those who have harmed them are devoid of responsibility. It is often helpful at this point to restate the definition of forgiveness and to clearly differentiate it from reconciliation. As the person injured by abuse engages in reframing and gains understanding, he/she also may begin to feel empathy (unit 13) and even compassion (unit 14) toward the offender. In actual practice, it has been observed that injured persons tend to experience more positive thoughts before they experience more positive feelings toward those who have harmed them. Knowledge of this point may be helpful to those who are struggling to see their abusers as imperfect, even suffering, humans and yet hold them accountable for their abusive behavior. As more positive thoughts and feelings emerge toward the abuser, the one harmed may come to recognize that he/she will need to absorb the pain of the injury in order to avoid passing it on to innocent others (unit 15). This unit does not imply denying or repressing one's pain, but rather a deliberate attempt to control any destructive expression of the pain so as to stop the cycle of abuse. This too may help one who has been abused to feel a sense of renewed control and even power as he/she chooses to contribute to a better future for both the self and others.

During the deepening phase of the forgiveness process, the abused may come to find meaning in his/her suffering (unit 16). This may come about through lessons learned about the self, others, or about life in general. The abused also may recognize that he/she has needed forgiveness at some time in the past (unit 17). Here again, it is important to emphasize that, while all people have needed forgiveness at some time, abuse survivors are never to be held responsible for the abuse itself. In other words, this unit does not suggest that the injured take responsibility for the abuse, but rather that the injured sees the self as a fallible human being. Unit 18 refers to the injured person's insight that he/she is not alone in the experience of suffering or on the forgiveness journey. Support may be found from friends, family members, fellow abuse survivors, and/or trained professionals. The abused may even discover a new purpose (unit 19) in life directly related to the injury such as counseling others who

and the forgiver can know a certain satisfaction in that he/she has chosen a response that hurts no one.

If the offender is willing and able to receive the gift of forgiveness offered then he/she also may experience healing. Reconciliation may then become a realistic goal. Of course, while forgiveness may pave the way to reconciliation, ultimately reconciliation will depend more on the trustworthiness of the offender than on the forgiveness offered. Nonetheless, even when reconciliation is impossible or unwise, the injured will find that in offering the gift of forgiveness, he/she receives a gift as well, the gift of healing.

REFERENCES

Al-Mabuk, R. H., Enright, R. D., & Cardis, P. A. 1995. Forgiveness education with parentally love-deprived late adolescents. *Journal of Moral Education*, 24: 427-444.

Benson, C. K. 1992. Forgiveness and the psychotherapeutic process. *Journal of Psychology and Christianity,* 11(1): 76-81.

Bergin, A. E. 1988. Three contributions of a spiritual perspective to counseling, psychotherapy, and behavior change. *Counseling & Values,* 33: 21-31.

Close, H. T. 1970. Forgiveness and responsibility: A case study. *Pastoral Psychology,* 21: 19-25.

Coyle, C. T., & Enright, R. D. 1997. Forgiveness intervention with post-abortion men. *Journal of Consulting and Clinical Psychology,* 65: 1042-1045.

Cunningham, B. B. 1985. The will to forgive: A pastoral theological view of forgiving. *The Journal of Pastoral Care,* 39:141-149.

Droll, D. M. 1984. "Forgiveness: Theory and Research." Ph.D.diss., University of Nevada-Reno. Abstract in *Dissertation Abstracts International-B,* 45: 2732.

Enright, R. D., & the Human Development Study Group. 1991. The moral development of forgiveness. In *Handbook of moral behavior and development,* (ed.) W. Kurtines and J. Gewirtz, Vol. 1: 123-152. Hillsdale, NJ: Erlbaum.

Enright, R. D., & the Human Development Study Group. 1996. Counseling within the forgiveness triad: On forgiving, receiving forgiveness, and self-forgiveness. *Counseling and Values,* 40: 107-126.

Enright, R.D. 2001. *Forgiveness is a Choice.* Washington, DC: APA Life Tools.

Fitzgibbons, R. P. 1986. The cognitive and emotional uses of forgiveness in the treatment of anger. *Psychotherapy,* 23: 629-633.

Flanigan, B. 1987. Shame and forgiving in alcoholism. *Alcoholism Treatment Quarterly,* 4: 181-195.

Frankl, V. E. 1959. *The will to meaning: Foundations and applications of logotherapy.* NY: World Publishing House.

Freedman, S. R., & Enright, R. D. 1996. Forgiveness as an intervention goal with incest survivors. *Journal of Consulting and Clinical Psychology,* 64: 983-992.

Haber, J. 1991. *Forgiveness.* Savage, MD: Rowman & Littlefield.

Hebl, J. H., & Enright, R. D. 1993. Forgiveness as a psychotherapeutic goal with elderly females. *Psychotherapy,* 30: 658-667.

Hope, D. 1987. The healing paradox of forgiveness. *Psychotherapy,* 24: 240-244.

Hunter, R. C. A. 1978. Forgiveness, retaliation, and paranoid reactions. *Canadian Psychiatric Association Journal,* 23: 167-173.

Kiel, D. V. 1986, February. I'm learning how to forgive. *Decisions,* 12-13.

Kolnai, A. 1973-74. Forgiveness. *Proceedings of the Aristotelian Society,* 74: 91-106.

Lin, W. 2001. "Forgiveness as an Educational Goal within a Drug Rehabilitation Center." Ph.D. diss., University of Wisconsin-Madison.

McAllister, E. W. C. 1983. Christian counseling and human needs. *Journal of Psychology and Christianity,* 2: 50-60.

Neblett, W. R. 1974. Forgiveness and ideals. *Mind,* 83: 269-275.

North, J. 1987. Wrongdoing and forgiveness. *Philosophy,* 6: 499-508.

Patton, J. 1985. *Is human forgiveness possible?* Nashville, TN: Abingdon.

Smedes, L. B. 1984. *Forgive and forget: Healing the hurts we don't deserve.* New York: Harper & Row.

Smith, M. 1981. The psychology of forgiveness. *The Month,* 14: 301-307.

Trainer, M. F. 1981. "Forgiveness: Intrinsic, role-expected, expedient, in the context of divorce." Ph.D. diss., Boston University. Abstract in *Dissertation Abstracts International-B,* 45: 1325.

Veenstra, G. 1992. Psychological concepts of forgiveness. *Journal of Psychology and Christianity,* 11: 160-169.

Waltman, M. 2002. "The psychological and physiological effects of forgiveness education in male patients with coronary artery disease." Ph.D. diss., University of Wisconsin-Madison.

Webster's Dictionary of the English Language, 1983, s.v. "reconcile."

Worthington, E. L., & DiBlasio, F. A. 1990. Promoting mutual forgiveness within the fractured relationship. *Psychotherapy,* 2: 219-233.

When Forgiveness
Is Not the Issue in Forgiveness:
Religious Complicity in Abuse
and Privatized Forgiveness

Margaret F. Arms

SUMMARY. This article examines public and private (individual) aspects of forgiveness relating to abuse and the complicity of religious institutions in abuse by some theological formulations and doctrines. It argues that the real issue is not whether to forgive but how much the process involves individual and religious institutional truth telling. Drawing from the work of Desmond Tutu and Carter Heyward, the author suggests that public and private dimensions of truth telling are critical components of forgiveness. Without the public participation of religious institutions in truth telling about their own complicity, privatized forgiveness is diminished but may stand as an act of resistance. *[Article copies available for a fee from The Haworth Document Delivery Service: 1-800-HAWORTH. E-mail address: <docdelivery@haworthpress.com> Website: <http://www.HaworthPress.com> © 2002 by The Haworth Press, Inc. All rights reserved.]*

KEYWORDS. Abuse, public/privatized forgiveness, religious complicity, truthtelling, Tutu, Heyward, resistance

---

[Haworth co-indexing entry note]: "When Forgiveness Is Not the Issue in Forgiveness: Religious Complicity in Abuse and Privatized Forgiveness." Arms, Margaret F. Co-published simultaneously in Journal of Religion & Abuse (The Haworth Pastoral Press, an imprint of The Haworth Press, Inc.) Vol. 4, No. 4, 2002, pp. 107-128; and: *Forgiveness and Abuse: Jewish and Christian Reflections* (ed: Marie M. Fortune, and Joretta L. Marshall) The Haworth Pastoral Press, an imprint of The Haworth Press, Inc., 2002, pp. 107-128. Single or multiple copies of this article are available for a fee from The Haworth Document Delivery Service [1-800-HAWORTH, 9:00 a.m. - 5:00 p.m. (EST). E-mail address: docdelivery@haworthpress.com].

Journal of Religion & Abuse, Vol. 4(4) 2002
http://www.haworthpress.com/store/product.asp?sku=J154
© 2002 by The Haworth Press, Inc. All rights reserved.
10.1300J154v04n04_09

For abuse survivors, considerations of forgiveness occur in the context of the concrete and harsh reality of their experiences. The questions I have heard from survivors, in the over fifteen year's psychotherapeutic work with them, come with a compelling intensity reflective of the physical, emotional, mental, and spiritual assault on their integrity that their abuse has brought. Their questions assume the form and tone of a litany. Not infrequently, clients respond to their own questions to me with a variation on Jesus' request to God as he hung on the cross, *"Father, forgive them, for they do not know what they are doing."*[1] In the survivor's responses, however, Jesus' words become not a request for forgiveness but an angry, ironic, sometimes bitter, question more in the spirit of protest found in the lamentation psalms.

How, some asked, do you forgive your grandfather who used you as the conduit to friends whom he sexually molested, and who swore he had not thereby harmed you?[2] Another wondered whether she could or should forgive the man who date raped her after being told no, and then remarked that her "no" was really a joke. Survivors of clergy sexual abuse questioned whether they could forgive their pastors who used the power of their office and position to molest survivors who came to help. These survivors had profound reservations about forgiving the institutional church that had known about the abusive clergy, and had done nothing except effect a geographical cure. They challenged the appropriateness of forgiving a church that insists forgiveness is the duty of every Christian but will not examine its own complicity in a culture of violence and abuse. How, even, they asked, do you forgive a God who seems to insist that the church is right and who likewise expects forgiveness? So go the questions for those who have experienced abuse. In the face of such experiences, perhaps the more meaningful question is yet another question: "Should we forgive?"

Forgiveness is a multilayered subject, with profound ethical issues surrounding decisions about the ability or advisability of abuse survivors to engage in the process of forgiveness. This article argues that dimensions of public and private participation embedded in the process of forgiveness place constraints on the relevance or wisdom of forgiving. For example, issues of truthtelling, power, and the privatization of the forgiveness process (by which I mean pressures on individuals to forgive) in the face of public (in the case of this article, religious institutions) absence from the process all contribute to concerns surrounding the process of forgiveness.[3] This article maintains that the discourse and process around decisions relating to forgiveness are more important considerations than issues about whether or not an abuse survivor should or should not forgive.

I approach the subject of forgiveness from the perspective of one who has spent over 15 years working with abuse survivors, most of whom were victims of sexual abuse, first in my psychotherapy practice and now at The Shalom Center where we work with their spiritual issues and questions. The lens filtering my thoughts on forgiveness are the stories of those who have come to my office seeking healing from deep wounds associated with abuse. Sometimes these clients have sought to find ways to forgive; sometimes they have sought to find strength not to forgive in the face of pressures to forgive. In either case, they have sought a path that has integrity both to the deep wounds caused by the people who harmed them and to their need to release the hold the abuse continued to have on their lives.

Axiomatic to the ensuing discussion of forgiveness is the clear claim that abuse is never, in any circumstance, justified. Abuse calls for a religious institutional response of challenge and confrontation of the acts and of the assumptions of power inherent in those acts. In short, abuse calls for firm resistance, or "no," from both a religio-cultural and an individual level. This article further assumes that if truthtelling is not possible, because it is dangerous for the abuse survivor, or because the abuse survivor is not ready to tell the truth about what happened, or because the offender (institutional or individual) declines to tell the truth, forgiveness cannot have integrity.

With the above in mind, this exploration of forgiveness vis à vis abuse approaches the subject from several angles. First, it begins by mapping the terrain and providing some of the various ways some scholars use the term "forgiveness." Second, it looks at the dimensions and process of truthtelling as the *sine qua non* of forgiveness. To make such a claim is not to suggest that truthtelling is the only aspect of forgiveness, it is, however, to claim that forgiveness cannot proceed without it. Without truthtelling, forgiveness becomes another way to maintain the "shameful secret," and a quick, superficial, albeit meaningless "fix." Furthermore, truthtelling requires the support of public, such as religious, institutions through their participation in the truthtelling process itself. Without such support, the danger of the process is too great for the abuse survivor.

Third, I examine the limitations placed on the private dimensions of forgiveness, by the religious institution's disengagement from the process. This article argues that religious institutions (the "public" aspect) often are complicit in individual acts of violence. At times, religious institutions are themselves primary offenders, such as explicit abuse by church professionals like those that have come to public awareness with the recent exposé of child molestation by Roman Catholic priests. Although clergy sexual abuse is devastating to those who are its victims and represents a flagrant and reprehensible act of abusive power, it is not the focus of this article.

A more subtle and common form of complicity in a violent and abusive culture exists in some religious doctrines and practices. For example, the public discussions about how many offenses ("strikes") will be tolerated before offending Roman Catholic clergy are removed from the priesthood strongly suggests that the Roman Catholic institution has some ambivalence about the nature of the offense.[4] Certainly, this ambivalence and reluctance to embrace a zero tolerance policy gives subtle, although presumably unintentional, room for abuse–at least once This more subtle variety of collusion with individual acts of abuse is the focus of the discussion below about the public religious institutional complicity in our culture of violence and abuse.

Another example of religious complicity in a culture of abuse takes the form of pressures on individuals to forgive abusive acts. Religious leaders and institutions pressure individuals (the "private" dimension) to forgive without engaging in institutional truthtelling about their own collusion with violence. In other words, the religious pressure is on the individual to forgive; but the religious institution absents itself from the process of truthtelling about its own contributions to abuse.[5] The process of forgiveness thus becomes privatized, and secret. These public and private dimensions of forgiveness draw the discussion towards consideration of the power dynamics inherent in acts of forgiveness.

Finally, this article claims that the real issue surrounding forgiveness in the face of abuse is less whether or not one forgives, but whether one engages the questions of forgiveness through truthtelling, an engagement that becomes an act of prophetic resistance. Preoccupation with forgiveness may detract from larger questions of religious complicity in perpetuating an abusive and violent climate that fosters individual acts of abuse. The conclusion is that forgiving or refusing to forgive both may be acts of resistance to abuse, depending upon the degree of truthtelling in the process. Engaging the questions and process surrounding issues of forgiveness with a stance of prophetic truthtelling then become the point of resistance to that abuse.

MAPPING THE TERRAIN

Defining forgiveness is a difficult task. The subject is complex, as numerous pastoral theologians who have attempted definitions can attest. For example, pastoral theologian David Augsburger in his book *Helping People Forgive* required 27 propositions to explain what he means by forgiveness.[6] Some argue that forgiveness is the giving up of hate and fantasies of revenge.[7] Others suggest forgiveness is a process tied to reconciliation and the "restoration of communion with God, with one another, and with the whole Creation."[8] Theologian Martin Marty suggests that forgiveness be understood "not so much as a doctrine . . . but as an ethos" emerging from the character of

God, which we as God's creation are to emulate.[9] Others, such as pastoral theologian Joretta Marshall, emphasize the importance of extending the process of forgiveness to include attention to aspects of communal complicity and participation in the wrongdoing.[10] All argue that forgiveness is hard work; none argues that forgiveness involves condoning harmful acts or forgetting.

Carter Heyward, in her book *Saving Jesus From Those Who Are Right,* offers a workable definition of forgiveness that includes many of the foregoing components of forgiveness, and allows for a focus on public and private truthtelling, the process central to the claims about forgiveness in this article. For that reason, her thinking about forgiveness is helpful. She writes, "Forgiveness is a social, political, and psychospiritual leap out of the past toward the future. It is a passage through obsessions with wrongs done. Even in small ways, it is a radical political act because it is the work of justice-love."[11] It is a definition suited to the purposes of this article because it focuses on forgiveness as a process intricately bound up with systems as well as individuals.

TRUTHTELLING:
THE VITAL INGREDIENT

The work of Anglican Archbishop Desmond Tutu is helpful in exploring the import of truthtelling vis à vis forgiveness.[12] His experience with the South African Truth and Reconciliation Commission, which was commissioned by the Mandela South African government in 1995 to bring healing and reconciliation to a nation decimated by the atrocities of apartheid, provides fertile ground for an examination of forgiveness in the ways outlined above.[13] The Truth and Reconciliation Commission was charged "to establish as complete a picture as possible" of what happened in the crime of apartheid.[14] The process went beyond a casual "This is what I did and I'm sorry." It examined both contextual factors as well as the individual crimes associated with apartheid. It involved exquisite attention and respect to the victims and their stories. The goal of the Truth and Reconciliation Commission was restorative rather than retributive justice.

As a secular structure and process, the South African parliament opted to use the language of "amnesty" rather than "forgiveness"; however, Tutu frequently uses the two terms interchangeably.[15] His work provides profound and relevant insights, especially in his insistence on the centrality of truthtelling as a prerequisite for forgiveness. Unlike the South African experience, the religious climate in the United States does not foster truthtelling on a religio-cultural level. This failure of religious and cultural truthtelling, especially on a religious level, undermines and limits the process of forgiveness.

rity then, it cannot be equated with forgetting. Survivors of abuse experience deep distress when religious leaders present forgiveness as a kind of cosmic spiritual eraser. Again, Tutu is helpful: Truthtelling is not forgetting. "In forgiving, people are not being asked to forget. On the contrary, it is important to remember . . . forgiveness does not mean condoning what has been done. It means taking what happened seriously and not minimizing it . . . "[22]

Furthermore, forgiveness, if it is to be a process of truthtelling, cannot be a return to the *status quo ante,* an impossibility because as an experience of trauma, abuse by its very nature disrupts and changes the ways its survivors experience the world. As rape survivor Ellen Halbert writes, "Overall it's pretty simple: everything in your life changes! Everything is turned upside down . . . [N]othing is ever the same again."[23] For others, there is no "ante": abuse has been the foundational, formative environment.

What people who have experienced abuse know is that life does not go back to before what happened; rather abuse survivors continue on knowing what happened changed their lives. Heyward does not define forgiveness as a leap to the past before the past, which is a form of forgetting; she defines it as a leap toward the future.[24] She is correct: forgiveness does not make what happened not have happened; nor does it blot out what happened as if it had not happened. In South Africa, Tutu writes, "we could not pretend that it [the atrocities of apartheid] had not happened."[25]

TRUTHTELLING AS REPENTANCE

Truthtelling by individual offenders and the complicit institutions requires careful and complete acknowledgment of what they have done and of their responsibility for the wrongdoing and the harm to the victim. Before they can leap out of the past, victims and offenders have to speak and hear the truth about that past. Furthermore, if truthtelling is to be a genuine leap toward the future, it must be heard from the perspective and privilege of the one(s) harmed. In other words, the confessional truth of the offenders needs to be heard in a climate that is clear about the depth of the individual abuse and also the complicity of the larger religious institutions in the supporting the offense. Otherwise, truthtelling become an exercise in rationalizations and justification of abuse. Truthtelling requires this step.

For example, a client's father, despite repeated requests to do so, refused to acknowledge responsibility for failing to keep his daughter safe from his sexually abusive brother.[26] This same father pled with my client, in my presence, for forgiveness. He acknowledged that he knew that his brother "liked" and was very "affectionate" with little girls, and admitted that he felt uncomfortable around his alcoholic brother. Ignoring the implications of this knowledge, the father continued to invite his brother to babysit my client after his brother lost his job over an "incident" with a coworker's daughter. Despite acknowledging his knowledge about his brother's suspicious behavior, my client's father denied any responsibility for failing to keep her safe. He wanted forgiveness, but would neither hear nor acknowledge the truth of his own complicity in his daughter's abuse. Another client told me of "orders" from her abusive older brother to forgive him because she is a "good Christian." This brother sought to restore family relationships without engaging in the hard work of truthtelling repentance. In such contexts, forgiveness holds integrity for neither the harmed nor the ones who did the harm.

Again, Tutu is instructive. He is clear that truthtelling requires acceptance of responsibility for harm, and is a vital component of forgiveness. "It is crucial," he writes, "when a relationship has been damaged or when a potential relationship has been made impossible, that the perpetrator should acknowledge the truth and be ready and willing to apologize."[27] Thus, difficult issues–of remembering, of accountability, of acknowledging wrongdoing in specificity, of accepting responsibility, of showing evidence of repentance through concrete behavior changes–weave through the process of truthtelling as a step towards forgiveness that heals rather than furthers the abuse.

The experience in South Africa was a mutual process between victim and offender that included three critical components of truthtelling about apartheid: cultural/societal truthtelling, perpetrator truthtelling, and victim truthtelling. Individual victims were not always matched to their own perpetrators. Because, however, individual truthtelling occurred within a context of national ownership and responsibility for the wrongs of apartheid, the process itself did not perpetuate the wrongs. In other words, the public commitment and participation in the process of truthtelling enabled rather than subverted private individual truthtelling.

PUBLIC DIMENSIONS:
RELIGIOUS COMPLICITY IN ABUSE

Contrasted to the South African experience with truthtelling and reconciliation, the situation in the United States offers little religio-cultural truthtelling or ownership of the violence endemic in abuse situations. Pastoral theologian James Poling writes that evil, within which category abuse certainly falls, is always both individual and communal. He argues that "three interlocking systems [are] necessary for genuine evil to be fully actualized-personal, social and religious evil."[28] The question might be raised, then, as to whether forgiveness on a privatized, individual level only reinforces the social and religious sanc-

the possibility of meaningful forgiveness in such circumstances is profoundly misleading.

To explore fully what truthtelling on a religious institutional level might involve is beyond the scope of this article, but some illustrations might prove helpful. Truthtelling begins as confession. Because of the litigious nature of our U.S. system, to expect truthtelling as I presented it in this article before legal questions are settled is probably unrealistic.[43] Nevertheless, below are some examples of what religious truthtelling might entail. Some are not relevant in court litigation and nothing prevents their enactment.

Religious truthtelling might include a public discussion about why abuse is evil, and not just sinful, and acknowledge that religious institutions have been complicit by not recognizing in language that abuse is evil. Religious truthtelling might include confession of co-optation of language and involve training clergy to explore with survivors of abuse why they use the language of evil rather than of sin. Religious truthtelling might confess that at times church institutions have been more concerned about institutional preservation than with confronting unethical behavior and holding abusive clergy accountable. Religious truthtelling might commit to engaging in a rigorous and public process of justice in its own house in the face of clergy abuse. It might confess the collusion with abuse that some of its doctrines (such as the atonement) support, and commit to a reexamination of those doctrines. Finally, a process of religious truthtelling might acknowledge that when religious institutions trivialize the profound depth of pain of abuse, as for example in ways discussed in this article, those religious institutions place themselves, however unintentionally, firmly in the mindset of offenders. To engage in religious institutional truthtelling thusly, would be a large step towards a meaningful and public process of forgiveness that would provide the religio-cultural integrity to facilitate private forgiveness.

PRIVATIZED FORGIVENESS AS RESISTANCE

In some ways, the foregoing considerations of religious complicity in abuse, that are inherent but rarely explicitly addressed in discussions of forgiveness, appear to leave people who have been abused with little means of releasing the hook of abuse. If to forgive may be meaningless as well as dangerous because of larger religious institutional failures to engage in truthtelling, is forgiveness then never appropriate? The complicity of religion, through its practices and doctrines, in a culture of violence and abuse seems to preclude individual forgiveness entirely. Short of a cultural acknowledgment and truth-telling about the institutional and societal complicity in violence, it is valid to question the appropriateness of engaging in forgiveness.

On the other hand, sometimes victims of abuse recognize all of the above dimensions of religious complicity in veiling the truth, know the unrepentant stance of the offender, and still wish to forgive. To insist that she or he cannot forgive is clearly insensitive, and might itself be considered power abuse. A more helpful response is to explore carefully and fully what forgiveness does not and cannot mean in such cases. Many victims struggle to undertake a process of forgiveness that has integrity, but does not collude with, perpetuate, or reinforce cultural, religious, and individual abuse. In other words, they seek to reconfigure privatized forgiveness so it releases them from the ties to abuse, yet confronts the offender and religious institutions with the harm done. Without accomplishing these latter tasks, any "forgiveness" reeks of lightly touching deep wounds. Consideration of these issues concludes this article.

The Unrepentant Offender and Privatized Forgiveness

Sometimes abuse survivors hope that private, or unilateral, forgiveness will in and of itself change their offender. Both Heyward and Tutu are clear that such thinking is an illusion. Heyward writes, "When we have no remorse for our wrongdoing or perhaps do not believe we have done wrong and therefore are not repentant, we cannot accept forgiveness. . . we place ourselves beyond the experience of forgiveness."[44] In such cases she insists, the offender places himself or herself even beyond God's "forgiving power."[45] Tutu is equally firm and clear: "The culprit may be arrogant, obdurate, or blind; not ready or willing to apologize or to ask for forgiveness. He or she thus cannot appropriate the forgiveness that is offered. Such rejection can jeopardize the whole enterprise."[46]

The point both theologians make is that no room or motivation to change exists if the offender (whether an individual or an institution) sees no fault in his/her/its behavior, exhibits and expresses no repentance or remorse, and shows no change in behavior. Offenders may see a need for reconciliation, but not repentance or remorse or change on their part. Through their denial, then, these offenders block the mutual process of forgiveness, which requires truthtelling. In such cases, privatized individual forgiveness cannot effect change in the offender (individual or corporate) or lead to forgiveness because no truthtelling occurs. The victim who "forgives" an unrepentant offender in the hopes of changing the offender and establishing a meaningful relationship is endangering himself or herself at worst or, at the very least, is setting the stage for deep disappointment.

Because privatized forgiveness is a unilateral rather than mutual process, it cannot change an unrepentant offender or restore a broken relationship or heal the harm of an individual offender. It cannot heal the harm caused by a religious institution that is complicit with abuse and violence. In neither case can it make the leap which Heyward argues is the essence of forgiveness. Paradoxically however, in certain circumstances, it might be a statement of resistance to abuse and violence.

Dimensions of Resistance in Privatized Forgiveness

Feminist ethicist and theologian Wendy Farley argues that in the face of evil, in which category I have placed abuse, the only empowering response is resistance: "Tragic suffering [her term for evil] cannot be atoned for; it must be defied."[47] To focus on whether individual victims should forgive their abusers becomes not only moot, but also perhaps a red herring. In the absence of religious institutional participation in the process of truthtelling as a component of forgiveness, the more meaningful concern is the extent to which victims are able to engage in truthtelling as resistant defiance of abuse, and to raise to public awareness and discourse attempts to privatize forgiveness. A caveat is important however: Just as forgiveness requires the support of a community, so too does resistance. It is risky indeed to attempt resistance alone.

Although privatized forgiveness is meaningless as a mutual leap to the future for the reasons discussed above, the *process* of forgiveness can constitute defiance and resistance to abuse and violence. Given the reality of religious complicity in fostering a climate that tolerates and even reinforces continued violence and abuse, the issue for victims is less whether they forgive but rather the extent to which victims engage the process, through truthtelling. In short, either forgiving or refusing to forgive can be an act of prophetic resistance. It needs to be reemphasized, however: neither choice (to forgive or not to forgive) can be made in isolation. Both decisions need the support and solidarity of a community of supporters.

Forgiveness as prophetic resistance. The slave gospel spirituals are a wonderful precedence for what I have in mind here.[48] What appeared, on the surface, to be an example of subservient co-optation of slaves by their masters was, in reality, a powerful statement of resistance. Forgiveness, like the slave spirituals, can represent a form of resistance and empowerment. To argue thusly is to suggest that private unilateral forgiveness has integrity when taken from the stance of prophetic of resistance. However, and this is an important factor, forgiveness in this sense cannot be coerced. It retains integrity to the extent that it is an intentional choice.

To state clearly and truthfully to oneself and to others exactly what the harm being forgiven is, in all its multilayered facets, represents a clear prophetic voice of resistance. Forgiveness as an act of resistance includes clear explication of the complicity of religious doctrines and practices in the offenses that are being forgiven. Furthermore, forgiveness in this sense does not imply condoning the harm or releasing from accountability individual and institutional offenders. To explain forthrightly that forgiveness in this instance is not complete nor does it restore the relationship is likewise to make a prophetic stand of resistance.

Privatized forgiveness as prophetic resistance is a decision to let go of the hold of the past on an individual life and to let go of resentment. *It is not, however, a decision to forget or to reconcile or even perhaps to let go of anger.* Forgiveness in this sense may be quite the opposite. It may be a decision to continue to speak out about what happened, to become a victim advocate, to remember the abuse, to use anger to work against violence and abuse.

In such manner, privatized forgiveness becomes a public statement of an intentional choice to cut the bonds of the past. It brings the private process into the arena of public discourse, and therein lies its power. To engage the process of forgiveness thusly invites the larger cultural and religious community into a mutual process of truthtelling. In short, the invitation is to a cultural-religious institutional "leap . . . toward the future," to revisit Heyward's words.[50] Whether the individual and institutional offenders join in the leap depends upon whether they are willing to engage in truthtelling. Indeed, if forgiveness is approached as an act of truthtelling in the face of public and personal denial on the part of the institutional and individual offenders, and as an understanding of the limitations and parameters inherent in private acts of forgiveness, it can stand as an act of resistance to abuse. In such cases, the victim resists and the victim forgives.

Refusing forgiveness as prophetic resistance. Similarly, to refuse to extend private forgiveness stands as resistance in that it calls the institution and individual offenders to accountability, despite denials of fault. Many survivors of abuse, sensing that to speak of forgiveness in the face of denial is to make mockery of the experience of abuse, will choose to refuse to extend forgiveness. To refuse demands for forgiveness with clear explanation, both of the reasons for refusal and of the process of mutual truthtelling necessary to begin forgiveness, is an empowering act of resistance for the victim of abuse. As with the decision to forgive, the choice to not forgive invites individual and institutional participants in abuse to embark upon a process of mutual truthtelling.

Such refusal does not mean that the victim necessarily continues to carry a grudge against the perpetrator, nor does it mean that the victim continues to be bound to the violence. It simply means that, without full acknowledgement and truth telling about what happened and who was responsible, and without genuine expressions and actions of remorse, the mutuality necessary for forgiveness is absent. It does not mean that the victim is forever bound to the abuse.

In refusing to accede to requests to "forgive and move on" without the requisite truthtelling, survivors can begin to cut the ties to their abuse. It can be an empowering moment of release for those who have been abused. Survivors of abuse can hold out the hope that their perpetrators will some day be willing to engage in truth telling, but not be driven by that hope. In so doing, they can begin to let go of lifelong ties to abuse. They stand, then, in the place of prophetic resistance by engaging the question of forgiveness through truthtelling. They resist, but they do not forgive.

In the end, then, to focus on whether or not to forgive may obfuscate the issue facing abuse survivors, namely, how best to resist and confront individual acts of abuse and institutional enabling of that abuse. Instead, the more compelling question surrounding forgiveness is not whether to forgive, but whether the process involved in whichever choice is made enables or resists abuse. Truthtelling, resistance, and making public attempts at privatization of forgiveness, then, are the more crucial issues in forgiveness in the face of violence and abuse.

To have meaning as forgiveness, both public and private domains need to engage in mutual truthtelling in ways that mirror the public and private dimensions of the original wounds of abuse. In the U.S. culture, while individuals are encouraged to forgive, religious institutions rarely participate in the process of truthtelling about their own complicity in the culture of violence and abuse. This failure in the public domain limits the ability of forgiveness to be, in Heyward's words cited earlier, "a leap toward the future." Instead, in such a context, privatized forgiveness becomes at best a leap sideways. When, however, privatized forgiveness engages in truthtelling about the absence of mutual truthtelling, then the *process* of privatized forgiveness, can stand as resistance, regardless of whether or not the victim of abuse chooses to forgive. It can free the victim from the bonds of the past while continuing to take a stance of resistance. With integrity and power, whether or not the victim forgives, he or she can say to individual offenders and complicit religious institutions, "I am free of this, but you are not, and we are not reconciled."

NOTES

1. In presenting this and the following litany of questions, personally and concretely, I do not mean to mock one of Jesus' last sayings on the cross. (Lk 23:34) I offer it in the spirit of feminist ethicist and theologian Wendy Farley who reminds scholars "we cannot allow ourselves to forget that the reality of evil is not present in ideas but is born by the fragile bodies of utterly unique persons existing in concrete situations of

ambiguity, pain and betrayal." Wendy Farley, *Tragic Vision and Divine Compassion: A Contemporary Theodicy* (Louisville, KT: Westminster/John Knox Press, 1990) 52.

2. Although I will not repeat the response, *Forgive them, for they know not what they do?* it should be the understood echo in each of the following litany questions.

3. This is not to argue that other public institutions, such as for example the entertainment industry and the media, do not also enable abuse and violence. This article, however, focuses on religion and its institutions.

4. This is not to single out the Roman Catholic Church as the only offender in these cases. Protestant denominations, likewise, have experienced similar conversations about disciplining abusive clergy.

5. Details of religious complicity in abuse on the part of religious institutions appears later in this article.

6. David Augsburger, *Helping People Forgive* (Louisville, KT: Westminster/John Knox Press, 1996), 165-168.

7. Marietta Jaeger, "The Power and Reality of Forgiveness: Forgiving the Murderer of One's Child" in Robert D. Enright and Joanna North, eds. *Exploring Forgiveness* (Madison WI: University of Wisconsin Press, 1998), 12.

8. L. Gregory Jones, *Embodying Forgiveness: A Theological Analysis* (Grand Rapids MI: William B. Eerdmans Publishing Co, 1995), xii.

9. Martin E. Marty, "The Ethos of Christian Forgiveness" in Everett L. Worthington Jr., *Dimensions of Forgiveness: Psychological Research & Theological Perspectives* (Philadelphia: Templeton Foundation Press, 1998), 15.

10. Joretta Marshall, "Communal Dimensions of Forgiveness: Learning from the Life and Death of Matthew Shepard." *Journal of Pastoral Theology* 9:1999:49-61.

11. Carter Heyward, *Saving Jesus From Those Who Are Right: Rethinking What It Means to Be Christian* (Minneapolis: Fortress Press, 1999), 183.

12. Tutu is not the only, or even the first, to recognize the importance of truthtelling in the process of forgiveness. Marie Fortune, beginning with her work *Is Nothing Sacred: When Sex Invades the Pastoral Relationship* (Cleveland: Pilgrim Press, 1989, 1999), has long argued for the necessity of truthtelling in the process of forgiveness.

13. Desmund Tutu, *No Future Without Forgiveness* (N.Y.: Image Books, 1999).

14. TRC [Truth and Reconciliation Commission] Act, Section 3. Cited in Janet Cherry, Historical Truth: Something to Fight for. Charles Villa-Vicencio and Wilhelm Verwoerd, eds *Looking Back, Reaching Forward: Reflections on the Truth and Reconciliation Commission of South Africa.* (Cape Town South Africa: University of Cape Town Press, 2000), 134.

15. Tutu (1999) does not actually provide a precise definition of his use of the word "amnesty." He writes about it as the process outlined by the South African Parliament in the Promotion of National Unity and Reconciliation Act. (49) Amnesty was in no way automatic or blanket; it was restricted to politically motivated offenses, and generally, the proceedings were held publicly, unless the victims were too frightened to speak publicly. (49). The offender applied for amnesty, engaged in an intense process of truthtelling, which was supported by sources other than the offender, and then appeared before a panel of the Truth and Reconciliation Commission that determined whether the requirements for amnesty had been fulfilled. (28) Tutu notes that this process allowed for perpetrators of apartheid to return to participation in South African national life: "It was the carrot of possible freedom in exchange for truth and the stick was, for those already in jail, the prospect of lengthy prison sentences, and, for those still free, the probability of arrest and prosecution and imprisonment." (30)

16. Marie M. Fortune, *Is Nothing Sacred: When Sex Invades the Pastoral Relationship* (San Francisco: Harper, 1989), 46. Fortune, using the RSV edition of the Bible, cites the prophet Jeremiah who bewailed the abuses of the leaders of the people and spoke of God's anger at those who "treated the wound of my people lightly, saying "Peace, Peace,"when there is no peace." Jer 6:14.

17. The Truth and Reconciliation Commission did not explicitly equate amnesty with forgiveness, but in the sense of Heyward's definition cited above in the prior section ("a leap out of the past toward the future" see n.3 above), amnesty may be seen as a process of forgiveness.

18. Johnny de Lange, "The Historical Context, Legal Origins and Philosophical Foundation of the South African Truth and Reconciliation Commission," in Villa-Vicencio and Verwoerd, 24.

19. Tutu, 93. Tutu argues that all humans are created in the image of God. To treat them as less than created in God's image is "veritably blasphemous" and "like spitting in the face of God."

20. Heyward, 185.

21. Tutu, 29.

22. Tutu, 271.

23. Quoted in Howard Zehr, *Transcending: Reflections of Crime Victims.* (Intercourse, PA: Good Books, 2001), 168.

24. See n. 5 above.

25. Tutu, 19.

26. The "clients" discussed in this article are composites of numerous clients I have seen over the years. None cited here represents any single client.

27. Tutu, 269.

28. James Poling, *Deliver Us From Evil: Resisting Racial and Gender Oppression* (Minneapolis: Fortress Press, 1996) 119.

29. Further discussion of religious institutional truthtelling is on p. 21 below.

30. Feminist theologians Rebecca Chopp and Elisabeth Schussler Fiorenza both, in their separate works, write on the important power issues inherent in naming and in decisions about use of language. Rebecca Chopp, *The Power to Speak: Feminism, Language, God* (New York: Crossroad, 1991). Elisabeth Schussler Fiorenza, ed. *The Power of Naming: A Concilium Reader in Feminist Liberation Theology* (Maryknoll, N.Y.: Orbis Books, 1996).

31. Margaret F. Arms, "A Practical Pastoral Theology of Resistance to Evil: Praxis as it Relates to Epistemologies of Evil Among Clergy and Abuse Survivors" (Ph.D. diss., Iliff School of Theology and the University of Denver, 2001). The research was a qualitative study about ways a sample of survivors of sexual trauma and a second sample of clergy from four mainline Protestant denominations understand evil.

32. Arms, 96-108.

33. Feminist theologians Rebecca Chopp and Elisabeth Schussler Fiorenza both, in their separate works, write on the important power issues inherent in naming and in decisions about use of language. Rebecca Chopp, *The Power to Speak: Feminism, Language, God* (New York: Crossroad, 1991). Elisabeth Schussler Fiorenza, ed. *The Power of Naming: A Concilium Reader in Feminist Liberation Theology* (Maryknoll, N.Y.: Orbis Books, 1996).

34. Clinicians and psychological theorists have identified the tendency of offenders to minimize the impact of their abusive behaviors on their victims. See for example Judith Herman, *Trauma and Recovery: The Aftermath of Violence-From Domestic Abuse*

to Political Terror (Boston: Basic Books, 1992) and Roy F. Baumeister, *Evil: Inside Human Violence and Cruelty* (New York: W.H. Freeman & Co., 1997).

35. Rita Nakashima Brock and Rebecca Ann Parker, *Proverbs of Ashes: Violence, Redemptive Suffering, and the Search for What Saves Us.* (Boston: Beacon Press, 2001).

36. Brock and Parker, 44.

37. Brock and Parker, 45.

38. Brock and Parker, 45.

39. Brock and Parker, 213.

40. Tutu, 37. Botha was succeeded by F. W. de Klerk as President. It was de Klerk who opened the political process to the black South African parties and thereby paved the way for the election of Nelson Mandela as President in April, 1994. Tutu is not endeared with de Klerk either whom he says "spoiled" the apology he (de Klerk) made before the Commission "when he qualified it virtually out of existence." Tutu, 251.

41. James Poling, *The Abuse of Power: A Theological Problem* (Nashville: Abingdon Press, 1991), 94.

42. The comment was made to me in a private conversation many years ago. Sandra Felt, L.C.S.W. Private practice. Colorado Springs, CO.

43. See n. 9 above.

44. Some restorative justice programs begin to appear in our legal system, especially in connection with drug and alcohol offenses. Also, victim-offender reconciliation programs operate in some areas with some degrees of success.

45. Heyward, 190.

46. Heyward, 190.

47. Tutu, 269.

48. Farley, 29.

49. Arthur C. Jones' book *Wade in the Water: The Wisdom of the Spirituals* (Maryknoll, N.Y.: Orbis Books, 1993) is an exploration of this theme in African-American spirituals.

50. See n. 5 above.

REFERENCES

Arms, Margaret F. 2001. A practical pastoral theology of resistance to evil: praxis as it relates to epistemologies of evil among clergy and abuse survivors. Ph.D. diss., Iliff School of Theology and the University of Denver.

Augsburger, David. *Helping People Forgive.* Louisville, KT: Westminster/John Knox Press, 1996.

Baumeister, Roy F. *Evil: Inside Human Violence and Cruelty.* New York: H. Freeman & Co., 1997.

Brock, Rita Nakashima and Rebecca Ann Parker, *Proverbs of Ashes: Violence, Redemptive Suffering, and the Search for What Saves Us.* Boston: Beacon Press, 2001.

Chopp, Rebecca. *The Power to Speak: Feminism, Language, God.* New York: Crossroad, 1991.

Enright, Robert D. and Joanna North, eds. *Exploring Forgiveness.* Madison WI: University of Wisconsin Press, 1998.

Farley, Wendy. *Tragic Vision and Divine Compassion: A Contemporary Theodicy.* Louisville, KT: Westminster/John Knox Press, 1990.

Fortune, Marie M. *Is Nothing Sacred: When Sex Invades the Pastoral Relationship.* San Francisco: Harper, 1989.

Herman, Judith. *Trauma and Recovery: The Aftermath of Violence–From Domestic Abuse to Political Terror.* Boston: Basic Books, 1992.

Heyward, Carter. *Saving Jesus From Those Who Are Right: Rethinking What It Means to Be Christian.* Minneapolis: Fortress Press, 1999.

Jones, Arthur C. *Wade in the Water: The Wisdom of the Spirituals.* Maryknoll, N.Y.: Orbis Books, 1993.

Jones, L. Gregory. *Embodying Forgiveness: A Theological Analysis.* Grand Rapids MI: William B. Eerdmans Publishing Co, 1995.

Marshall, Joretta. Communal Dimensions of Forgiveness: Learning from the Life and Death of Matthew Shepard. *Journal of Pastoral Theology* 9: 1999:49-61.

Poling, James. *The Abuse of Power: A Theological Problem.* Nashville: Abingdon Press, 1991.

_____. *Deliver Us From Evil: Resisting Racial and Gender Oppression.* Minneapolis: Fortress Press, 1996.

Schussler Fiorenza, Elisabeth, ed. *The Power of Naming: A Concilium Reader in Feminist Liberation Theology.* Maryknoll, N.Y.: Orbis Books, 1996.

Tutu, Desmund. *No Future Without Forgiveness.* N.Y.: Image Books, 1999.

Villa-Vicencio, Charles and Wilhelm Verwoerd, eds. *Looking Back, Reaching Forward: Reflections on the Truth and Reconciliation Commission of South Africa.* Cape Town South Africa: University of Cape Town Press, 2000.

Worthington Jr, Everett L. *Dimensions of Forgiveness: Psychological Research & Theological Perspectives.* Philadelphia: Templeton Foundation Press, 1998.

Zehr, Howard. *Transcending: Reflections of Crime Victims.* Intercourse, PA: Good Books, 2001.

When Sisters Dream

Nancy Werking Poling

KEYWORDS. Abuse and forgiveness

In Hebrew Scriptures men usually got the exciting roles of patriarch and prophet. Wondering how some of the stories might have read had women been the protagonists, I've adapted a few, among them this one about Joseph. For women who have experienced betrayal and abuse at the hands of those they trust, the importance of this narrative may be that it speaks to the issue of forgiveness.

Some readers may benefit from the following summary of the story as told in Genesis 37-46:

Not only did Joseph's brothers resent his being their father's favorite, they grew tired of listening to his self-promoting dreams. Instead of killing him, which they seriously considered, they sold him into slavery then led their father to believe he'd been killed by a wild beast. Years later, when a famine came upon their land, the brothers traveled to Egypt. There they were surprised to meet Joseph, who was in charge of distributing food. Later, after their father Jacob died, the brothers asked for Joseph's forgiveness. Joseph's reply was that only God could forgive.

Around the well, in the grazing areas, none of us spoke of what had happened. It was as if she'd never lived.

But I had dreams. Not the kind she once had, but terrifying ones where her blood cried out and demanded revenge. Like it or not, I discovered, she was bound to us by blood.

[Haworth co-indexing entry note]: "When Sisters Dream." Poling, Nancy Werking. Co-published simultaneously in Journal of Religion & Abuse (The Haworth Pastoral Press, an imprint of The Haworth Press, Inc.) Vol. 4, No. 4, 2002, pp. 129-134; and: *Forgiveness and Abuse: Jewish and Christian Reflections* (ed: Marie M. Fortune, and Joretta L. Marshall) The Haworth Pastoral Press, an imprint of The Haworth Press, Inc., 2002, pp. 129-134. Single or multiple copies of this article are available for a fee from The Haworth Document Delivery Service [1-800-HAWORTH, 9:00 a.m. - 5:00 p.m. (EST). E-mail address: docdelivery@haworthpress.com].

Did my sisters dream? I dared not ask, for not only did we never mention Josepha, we didn't discuss dreams any more. Because the two were so closely connected, Josepha and dreams.

The Dreamer, we called her.

"You'll never guess what I dreamed last night." Each morning a dream more glorious than the one from the previous night. Each morning one that elevated Josepha above the rest of us. "We were binding sheaves in the fields—"

"When was the last time you bound sheaves? As I recall you're always having your period. As if that's reason enough for our precious little—"

"Judith!" our mother interrupted sharply. She would always come to Josepha's defense.

"Really, Mother, she never does her share of the work."

"I do too. Anyway, we were binding sheaves, and my sheaf rose and stood upright, and your sheaves gathered around it and bowed down to it."

Bedlam broke out among us, one sister hollering that even in her dreams Josepha was insufferable. Another shouting, "If I have to listen to one more of your high and mighty dreams, I'm going to cram a ram's horn down your throat!"

"Why can't you girls get along?" In Mother's voice we heard more a plea than a question.

But the next day was the same.

"You'll never guess what I dreamed last night."

"Another one where we all bow down to Your Majesty?" I asked with sarcasm.

Josepha lifted her chin proudly. "The sun, moon, and stars were bowing down to me."

The ten of us hooted. Only Bea, the youngest, sat there not understanding what the uproar was about. At least this time Mother scolded Josepha for her arrogance.

Unfazed by Mother's disapproval, she turned to leave the room. "Well, you can't blame a woman for what she dreams, can you?" The rest of us glared after her as she glided away in her colorful robe.

"Why don't the rest of us ever have dreams like that?" we asked each other later, as we sheared the sheep. As usual, Josepha had found some excuse not to help.

Asha said her dreams were filled with embarrassing situations, where her clothes fell off or she forgot how to do some ordinary task, such as how to draw water from the well.

Shy Dana confided that hers were dreams of the day. Sometimes she moved among the animals dreaming that she was conversing with ease, that she was witty and clever in speech.

Judith said nothing, but we all knew, because each night we took turns getting up when she screamed out. Then we would hold her in our arms as she sobbed, wanting her painful dreams to cease.

Neither did I speak. There had been a time when I, like Dana, had dreams of the day, where people admired my beauty or my accomplishments. Then as years passed, the demands of physical labor became too much, and I began to dream instead of escape–of a lover, a vast inheritance, any means of getting away I could think of. Until I knew such things would never come to pass, and I gave up dreams of the day altogether.

Those of us who feared our dreams or had abandoned them resented Josepha. It was as if she were empowered by hers, while the rest of us served as receptacles for dreams that either terrified us or left us without hope.

She was walking toward me, her colorful robe flapping in the wind, her arms outstretched as they so often were, as if she were embracing life. Standing at the foot of my mat, she shouted, "Why didn't you stop them?" Her tone was so loud that I wakened and could not go back to sleep.

At first my intent was simply to scare her, to rid her of her arrogance. My sisters, however, said, "Let's kill her and throw her into one of the pits." As Josepha crouched there at our feet, trying to protect her head with her arms, our blows became fiercer. The years of jealousy expressed themselves in a rage we could not control. It was Reba who finally admonished us not to kill Josepha, to instead throw her into a pit. Would we have killed her otherwise? I do not know.

"You're just jealous," Josepha called up to us, "because I'm going to do something with my life, while the bunch of you–none of you is ever going to amount to anything." I was surprised she still had the strength to speak.

"Why don't you take a nap down there–that rock will make a fine pillow–and then tell us about your dream." We all joined in raucous laughter.

Why didn't I stop them? How could I stop them when I couldn't even stop myself?

The beautiful robe walked toward me. No body was beneath its folds, yet it had form. I wanted it. I wanted to wear it and be admired. Closer it came, until I was able to reach out and possess it. But as I tried to put it on, it rose and began to wrap itself around my neck. I sat up with a start, gasping for breath.

I remember the look on her face as I tore the prized garment from her body. I remember the satisfaction I felt when I heard it rip. How I envied her that robe, a birthday gift from Mother, far surpassing any gift I ever received. The years I had tried to please Mother, practically worked my body to its death, and then for Josepha to find favor so easily. Mother's favorite, daughter of her late child-bearing years, the seed planted by her second husband, whom she loved far more than my father.

How easy it was to sell a sister into slavery. To exchange a young woman with extravagant dreams for a handful of silver coins. Watching the caravan journey on, we joked among ourselves, taking joy in her humiliation.

"Instead of being waited upon by the sun and moon and stars, she'll do the serving."

"She didn't share the burden of work at home, let her see now what work really is like in some distant city where people don't even speak her language. See if anyone there cares about her dreams."

"Oh, no, not my Josepha," Mother wailed when we showed her the robe, torn and splattered with a goat's blood. "Not my Josepha." When I saw how sobs racked her body so violently she could scarcely breathe, I rejoiced in what we had done; for I knew Mother never would have felt such sorrow over my death. Yet a trace of shame crept over me. Shame for making my mother cry, shame for betraying her trust in us.

All ten of us were implicated, so no one dared break the oath of silence. No one dared tell Mother that Josepha was not dead but had been sold as a slave. We let Mother assume the worst.

I was slaughtering a goat, smearing blood on the elegant robe, when suddenly the goat turned into Josepha, and she was wearing her robe, her own blood darkening its colors. Many years had passed since we'd sold her, but the dreams persisted.

We had new worries now, concerns about our family's welfare. For several years the winter rains had not come, leaving the fields parched. Without grass we could no longer keep livestock, and with neither grains nor animals we had little to eat. How I ached as I watched the children, who instead of playing their running games, sat quietly around Mother, their voices soft. We all knew we would not likely live to see another year.

"I hear there's grain in Egypt," Mother said one day. "Go down and buy some so we will live."

Carrying empty sacks and the money she had given us, we made the journey, all of us except Bea, who by now had replaced Josepha as Mother's favorite.

The sun made its way nearly all the way across the sky as we stood in line for grain. "Why did we go to all the trouble of making this journey?" we complained among ourselves. "Even if there is enough, the Egyptians probably won't sell to foreigners."

When we finally arrived at the front of the line, we bowed before the woman in charge, our faces to the ground. As soon as I looked up, I was intimidated. Her clothing was of the finest fabric, her jewelry expensive. Everything about her–the way she walked, talked, made decisions–everything indicated power.

How must I, a woman who walked among sheep and dressed in coarse material, look to one so fine? Surely, I reasoned, she came from an important family and had spent her life among the rich and powerful.

"Who are you?" she demanded.

"We are daughters of one woman, twelve of us. The youngest is home with our mother, and another is no more."

"You are spies," she accused us, her many bracelets jingling as she shook her hand in anger. "You have come to see how weak we have become."

"N-n-no," I stuttered, "we have come to buy grain."

The next three days were filled with confusion. The woman was intent upon seeing the youngest girl of the family. Why would Bea's appearance convince her we were not spies? At first she jailed all ten of us, then changed her mind, saying that if one of us remained as a hostage, the others could return home and bring Bea back with them. We left Sima behind.

At first Mother resisted our taking Bea back to Egypt. But as the famine worsened, we knew that unless we returned there we would die. And if we returned without Bea our pleas for food would be ignored.

I was perplexed by the powerful woman's reaction to seeing Bea. The lines on her face softened, her eyes grew misty. How startled I was when she began to weep. Startled yet more when she called through her sobs, "I am Josepha. Is my mother still alive?"

Disbelief–that was my initial reaction. Disbelief that she had survived our betrayal. Not just survived but prospered, accomplishing more than any of us could have–dare I say, *dreamed of*? We pretended to be overjoyed at this reunion, hugging and kissing and shrieking with delight. Pretended because we were, in fact, terrified. Her tactics with us–accusing us of being spies, putting us in jail, keeping Sima hostage until we brought Bea–all had been to show us the power she now had over our destiny. I thought back to her dream, the one in which her sheaf stood upright while ours bowed down to it, and recognized this was the event the dream foretold.

While she immediately assured us there would be no retaliation, I did not believe her. After all, we, her sisters, had renounced our kinship by selling her into slavery. We had sent her to a foreign land, far from her mother whom she loved, far from the traditions of her people. Yet she declared this a time of festivity. So while we all clung to each other and shouted words of joy, I was convinced that at any moment the festivities would suddenly stop and she would bring her wrath down upon us.

Instead she said, "Go now, bring Mother, so that our family will survive the famine."

There were, of course, initial apologies. Though offered with sincerity they were sprinkled with words of justification: "If you hadn't always been bringing up those egotistical dreams . . . At least we didn't kill you." And to our mother: "If you hadn't favored her . . . If you hadn't given her a robe far more beautiful than anything we had . . ."

Then came the tears. We wept uncontrollably over what we had done.

Our tears were for naught. Survival was at stake. Ours and our children's. Josepha's generosity was for them, she explained, for they had had nothing to do with the betrayal. She was committed to the continuation of the blood line.

It was not reconciliation, this arrangement we worked out. Our encounters were not without tension. In a businesslike manner Josepha made sure we had the food we needed, that our livestock was fed, that we occupied choice land. Only upon Mother and Bea did she shower affection.

Then Mother died. Though we all cried, Josepha wept the most. She and Mother had, after all, felt a closeness, which though resented by the rest of us, had enabled us to survive the famine. I think Josepha also, more than we, understood Mother's legacy and the significance of her generation passing.

But we were certain that with Mother's death Josepha would seek revenge. So we told another lie: "Before she died Mother told us to tell you that you are to forgive us the evil we did to you." It was the first time the word "forgiveness" had been spoken. I thought it an excellent strategy, for Josepha was certain not to go against Mother's wishes. And we had included *for the evil we did to you,* meaning we were acknowledging that what we had done was wrong. To make it harder for her to refuse, we fell down on our knees before her.

Josepha sat there weeping. Sorrowfully she shook her head no. "Only God can forgive," she finally said, "I cannot assuage your guilt. What you did to me *was* evil. God has used that evil for good, so that many people could be kept alive. Don't worry, I will continue to provide for you and your little ones. Only do not ask me to forgive you."

So we all continued to live together. But we could not undo what had been done.

I keep thinking of the importance of dreams. Dreams are full of mystery, for those that occur in the night come uninvited. Where do they come from? From God? Or do we create our own dreams? Both perhaps.

The mystery surrounding Josepha–murdered, according to the lie we told Mother. All because of her dreams. Yet that which inspired wrath and jealousy among us sisters became her salvation and the source of her power.

Is that perhaps how God turns evil ways to good? By keeping dreams of new possibilities alive?

The Practice of Forgiveness in Sue Miller's Novel *The World Below*

Jane McAvoy

SUMMARY. This article argues that literature rather than works in Christian theology or the social sciences provide the best resource for imagining the practice of forgiveness. *The World Below*, by Sue Miller is used as a case study to imagine the elements in a forgiving relationship. In this novel the lines between victim and offender are blurred and the actions of accountability are shaped by differences in gender and power. Memory places a crucial role as enabling forgiveness. The natural grace of remembering is the key to a theology that embodies the practice of forgiveness. *[Article copies available for a fee from The Haworth Document Delivery Service: 1-800-HAWORTH. E-mail address: <docdelivery@haworthpress.com> Website: <http://www.HaworthPress.com> © 2002 by The Haworth Press, Inc. All rights reserved.]*

KEYWORDS. Sue Miller, *The World Below*, religion and literature, forgiveness, memory, grace.

"This was who he was then. Betrayed, robbed by his wife, he tried to understand the reasons why she might have felt it necessary to do either and to arrange their lives so she'd never have to do it again."[1]

[Haworth co-indexing entry note]: "The Practice of Forgiveness in Sue Miller's Novel *The World Below*." McAvoy, Jane. Co-published simultaneously in Journal of Religion & Abuse (The Haworth Pastoral Press, an imprint of The Haworth Press, Inc.) Vol. 4, No. 4, 2002, pp. 135-148; and: *Forgivenss and Abuse: Jewish and Christian Reflections* (ed: Marie M. Fortune, and Joretta L. Marshall) The Haworth Pastoral Press, an imprint of The Haworth Press, Inc., 2002, pp. 135-148. Single or multiple copies of this article are available for a fee from The Haworth Document Delivery Service [1-800-HAWORTH, 9:00 a.m. - 5:00 p.m. (EST). E-mail address: docdelivery@haworthpress.com].

With this observation, Sue Miller invites her readers into an imaginary world that outlines the complexities of forgiveness. It is the kind of narrative that describes the relational nature of forgiveness by blurring the lines between victim and offender. It helps the reader to understand the importance of memory in the process of forgiveness. It tells the story of a forgiven and forgiving relationship. Through this process the reader is allowed to imagine the possibility and understand the complexity of forgiveness.

In the premier issue of *Journal of Religion & Abuse* Millicent Fiske argues that fictional narratives in which characters survive and even flourish in the face of oppression are fruitful sources for theological reflection. Such narratives help theologians to "envision new and alternative ways of imagining and articulating redemption." Their power comes not from imitating real life, but from the very utopian nature of fictional stories. By reaching beyond what our imaginations think is possible these narratives create an "enabling space within which our own partial attempts to fashion existences shaped by our desires for freedom, joy and love may be more easily and fully realized."[2] Thus they provide an eschatological source for theological reflection. By showing us what we hope is possible they enable us to envision what a healthy relationship should be and critique more clearly relationships that fall short of this vision.

Turning to a work of fiction may seem an unusual approach to understanding forgiveness, but it is needed, in part, because recent books in Christian theology have failed to provide much hope or vision for practicing forgiveness. One such effort is *Embodying Forgiveness* by Gregory Jones. Jones describes forgiveness as a craft or habit that Christians live out in their daily lives. The goal is to imitate Christ in bearing the cost of forgiveness in one's body and soul.[3] Likewise Miroslav Volf defines forgiveness as the will to embrace one's enemy in self-giving love. Like Jones, Volf turns to the event of the crucifixion as the archetype for forgiveness. The scandal of the cross is that self-giving love fails to overcome violence. The will to embrace the other precedes the truth about the other or the claim of justice. Forgiveness means that love, not freedom, is the ultimate goal of the Christian life.[4]

Certainly Jones and Volf are aware of the potential problems this interpretation of forgiveness may have for victims of abuse, and both are aware of feminist critiques of forgiveness; but their concern for comprehending the meaning of the crucifixion takes precedence over their fear that claims to bear the cross may be harmful for victims of abuse. The result is a theory of forgiveness that comprehends the whole of the Christ event, but fails to offer hope to the lives of a great majority of their readers. Ivone Gebara notes "the very epistemology that reveals evil and denounces it can also produce it by obscuring certain aspects of human reality."[5] In the work of Jones and Volf, the very epistemology that turns to the cross to reveal God's triumph of embrace over exclusion can exclude and damage those most in need of God's care.[6]

It is this failure to cohere with the reality of daily life that has led studies in the social sciences to dismiss the practice of forgiveness. Philosopher Aurel Kolnar labels forgiveness unjustified or pointless. If it is given without restitution it is unjust, if restitution has been made then forgiveness is not needed. Either way the discussion of forgiveness is a moot point. Forgiveness is illogical.[7] Another concern is whether forgiveness is a healthy response. Ruth Kluger notes that however much we say that to forgive is not to forget, the reality is that our minds link the ability to remember with resentment and forgetfulness with forgiveness. Since the mind is wired to remember, humans treat forgetfulness as a sickness and should consider forgiveness in the same category.[8]

The most troubling critique is the dismissal of forgiveness as a useless fiction. Scholars are not necessarily speaking of the Christian tendency to link forgiveness with the crucifixion, but the more general religious claim that forgiveness is a super-human activity, the work of God. Martha Minnow's study on vengeance and forgiveness notes that forgiveness requires the belief in transcendence that, by definition, cannot be achieved on command. Forgiveness is an act of grace, the work of God. Thus from her legal perspective forgiveness is not a viable concept since it cannot be mandated or achieved by human systems.[9] Cary Nelson notes that the refusal of forgiveness is not just the refusal to forget, but also the rejection of the ideology of transcendence and the false public fiction of rebirth.[10]

Despite these doubts, some scholars have taken a new interest in forgiveness. One such effort is the International Forgiveness Institute, which has developed a forgiveness inventory and outlined a twenty-step process of forgiveness.[11] The Institute has conducted numerous scientific studies on the healing benefits of forgiveness. One such study correlates the marital adjustment of women who have suffered child abuse with their forgiveness inventory scores. Those with higher scores of forgiveness have happier marriages.[12] Their conclusion is that forgiveness reduces stress, anxiety, grief, and depression as well as increases hopes and emotional well-being. The Institute argues that forgiveness is possible; and those who forgive lead happier, healthier, psychologically sound, and socially adjusted lives.

Philosopher and psychologist, Julia Kristeva, challenges the scientific community not to ignore the religious dimensions of forgiveness, but instead to embrace the faith stance upon which it is based. She argues for considering the possibility of transcendence and the hope of rebirth. Forgiveness is "the ability to give meaning beyond non meaning," to provide an interpretation of events that transcends suffering by opening it up to "something else." This quest for rebirth is a psychological process that happens in the private, not the public realm.[13] By separating the personal from the political, Kristeva notes that justice is a public matter that may be pursued alongside the private need for forgiveness, but should not be confused with it. Forgiveness may or may not coexist with justice. The separation of the two clarifies the place and the process of both.

This brief sampling of forgiveness studies shows the longing for the practice of forgiveness and the complexity of imagining it. Theological studies try to imagine the truth of the Christian story but have a hard time reconciling the potential dangers of unjust relationships with the witness of Christ's life. Scientific studies give helpful critiques that challenge assumptions about the assumed benefits of forgiveness, but raise questions about what should stand in the place of the hope for transcending unforgiving relationships. Those that do advocate the practice of forgiveness offer only the hope of a well-adjusted existence. If we accept the central claim of theologians like Jones and Volf that forgiveness is the heart of the good news and the suggestion of philosophers like Kristeva that we should embrace the hope of a rebirth that transcends suffering, then how might we imagine the practice of forgiveness?

The need to imagine forgiveness anew suggests a turn to narratives of forgiveness. Literary critic, Wayne Booth, suggests that narratives expand our imaginations by offering new roles that we take on to imagine who we are or might become. Narratives have the benefit of introducing us to "the practice of subtle, sensitive moral inference, the kind that most moral choices in daily life require of us." The point is not to search for the perfectly moral character, but to look at the moral sensitivity of the author of the narrative who "insists I see what these people (the characters of the story) are doing to each other."[14] Good narratives are ones in which the author describes a comprehensive view of life that displays grounds for responsible choices and motives for moral laws. At the same time a good narrative provides a correspondence with our experience in a way that resonates with our lives by showing us the capacity for nobility and the remedy for vice.[15]

Sue Miller's novels have been so popular because of the depth of her moral sensitivity. Her books are reviewed in the *New York Times* as well as the *Christian Century* for her exploration of the themes of faith and grace in domestic relationships. One reviewer has noted that she is a master of rendering the "weave and texture, the tonality of everyday life."[16] Another writes that Miller stands alongside John Updike and Frederick Buechner as a master of writing about the trials of faith.[17] Miller herself acknowledges the ethical dimension of her narratives. In a recent interview she notes that her Christian upbringing gives her a tendency toward "self-examination and the examination of others–intentions, meanings, scruples, (and) ethics."[18]

Miller's novels do an excellent job of describing the various forms of abuse that affect family systems and the difficulty of forgiving those who do you harm. Her characters tend to be nice people who do not kill or rape each other but engage in "subtle" forms of family abuse such as verbal belittling and emotional control. It is this ability to develop likeable characters that makes the depiction of their abusive ways so revealing. In *The Good Mother*, the reader is drawn into the world of a well-meaning mother who is accused of exposing her child to sexual abuse; but the evidence suggests this is a false accusation. The child's father sues for custody and refuses to consider any form of forgiveness. The reader is left to decide how the child will be affected by this decision.

In her next novel it is the child who forgives her parents. *Family Pictures* describes the struggles of a couple with an autistic son. While the wife can never forgive her husband for his assumption that she was responsible for their son's illness, their daughter learns to forgive both parents for "what they can't forgive in each other."[19] In this novel the reader is left longing for the couple to forgive each other, but Miller's next novel makes one question whether forgiveness is a worthy goal. *For Love* compares the relatively good life of a daughter who refuses to forgive her physically abusive mother, with the emotionally troubled life of the seemingly good and forgiving son. The daughter's son notes that one "can't forgive unless you let go of the 'gravity of everything'[20] and the reader wonders if some things should not be let go. The lesson of this novel is that the pretense of forgiveness is more damaging to the victim and less moral than honest resentment.

Forgiveness becomes a more prominent theme in Miller's later novels. *The Distinguished Guest* describes the relationship of a delightfully energetic, but verbally abusive, elderly woman and her adult son. He forgives his mother for her hurtful remarks, but only after her death. Having given her readers a look at the possibility of forgiveness, Miller's next novel suggests even faithful people do not easily achieve it. *While I Was Gone* explores the temptation of an extra-marital affair. While the wife resists the affair, her husband (who is a local pastor) cannot forgive her for even considering this act of betrayal. Miller's portrayal of a minister who can preach the gospel but not forgive his wife seems to raise the question of what kind of faith is needed to foster a forgiving heart.

It is only in her latest novel that Miller develops a forgiving relationship. *The World Below* tells the story of the passions and actions that lie below the surface of the early 20th century marriage of John and Georgia Holbrooke. The story centers on a misunderstanding about John's offer to forgive Georgia for being "damaged goods" at the time of their wedding. Georgia makes this confession to acknowledge that she had a pre-marital affair with a young man while she was in a sanitarium recovering from tuberculosis. John mistakenly thinks she is confessing to having a body damaged by disease. Only later is the truth revealed when Georgia confesses her grief over her former lover's death. John admits that knowing about her affair changes everything and he does not know if he can forgive Georgia. During a heated exchange Georgia discovers that John (who was her doctor during her illness) had her committed to a sanitarium, not because he knew it would heal her, but because he hoped it would break the ties with her father, make her receptive to his offer of marriage, and essentially alter the entire course of her life. "You had no right to do that," she says.[21] For two days they do not speak.

· In the months that follow, Georgia and John resume their lives without mentioning their disagreement. All the while, Georgia secretly takes money from the household budget to pay for her former lover's funeral expenses. After attending the burial she confesses her subterfuge to John and declares that this is the end of her old love and old life. This time John does not erupt in anger, but tries to imagine how to be the generous and forgiving person Georgia had mistakenly thought him to be. His response is to open a bank account in her name, an unprecedented act of financial freedom for the early 1920s.

Georgia's granddaughter, Catherine, tells this story. When Catherine pieces together the details of their lives, she recognizes her grandfather's act as a noble gesture that would free her grandmother from his control. Catherine concludes, "This was who he was then. Betrayed, robbed by his wife, he tried to understand the reasons why she might have felt it necessary to do either and to arrange their lives so she'd never have to do it again."[22] Or was it an act that reestablished balance and paid restitution for changing her life? Or was it just keeping up with the times of women's emerging rights? Catherine lays all these options before the reader and then concludes, "I wept for everything that must have been painful for both of them in all this."[23]

Miller does a masterful job of drawing the reader into the complexity of this relationship through Catherine's growing awareness. Catherine, in the role of narrator, tells us how her grandmother's memory of the bank account and her time in the sanitarium compares with the stories Catherine has heard from other relatives and the knowledge Catherine pieces together from reading her grandmother's diaries and house ledgers. As she tells the story to Catherine, Georgia stresses her husband's generosity, but makes no mention of errors on her own part that need to be forgiven. But as Catherine puzzles over the diaries she sees a deeper picture. "I could feel her in that careful record," Catherine states, "I could imagine her voice expanding the compressed version I was reading. I could imagine her way of telling the story."[24] The story of forgiveness emerges as Catherine's imagination fills in the details and gives us a fictionalized account of her grandparent's actions and feelings.

This fictionalized memoir draws the reader in as fellow observer of the process of forgiveness. As Catherine compares the lack of forgiveness in her own failed marriages with her grandparent's forgiving marriage, we are invited to compare our own relationships with this fictionalized account. Catherine remembers how her grandmother compared the shame, failure, and loss that she felt when she had tuberculosis with Catherine's shame, failure, and loss of her husband's love. Catherine notes that Georgia's life was "running steady as a buried stream under mine."[25] As one commentator notes, the marriage of John and Georgia is "the kind readers hunger to read about."[26] In its quest for freedom and equality it is a modern marriage; in its angst over the loss of virginity it is old-fashioned. The reader wonders along with Catherine how it is possible to build a life-long relationship that forgives broken trust.

The key to this story is the identification of Georgia as "damaged goods." The damage to her reputation is done by her affair with a fellow patient in the sanitarium. While there Georgia feels that she is transported to a future world of sexual freedom. But she returns home to a world where sexual mores require female virginity. When John accepts her apology, albeit misunderstanding the meaning of the phrase "damaged goods," she feels that she is more than goods, damaged or otherwise. Her decision to use household money for her own purposes is further proof that she will not accept the assigned role as her husband's property.

While one might assume that Catherine's sympathies would be with her grandmother's efforts to break out of the gender restrictions of her day, she instead shows the reader how her grandfather understood this behavior as self-centered insensitivity. It is a self-consciousness based on a blunt honesty that he has come to love. For the sake of retaining his relationship with this honest and modern woman, he realizes the damage he had done by sending her to the sanitarium under false pretenses. While talking with Catherine, he confesses that he had too much power over his wife's life. He tries to restore the power balance by giving his wife her own money, but it takes the rest of their marriage to undo the damage done by the loss of her freedom.

The World Below is a story that recognizes the power differences between men and women and the way in which these differences set up situations of control and loss. While the relationship is not physically abusive, it exhibits the desire for control through manipulation of resources and emotions that harm the other. Forgiveness comes through acknowledging this power to control, the ability to change another's life for good and ill, and the loss of freedom that results from the exercise of self will. The process of forgiveness involves understanding the damaging effects of one's own power, acknowledging the other's loss, and offering compensation that, in part, restores lost freedom. It is important to note here the different kinds of compensation required by both parties. John, in control of their public lives, gives up control over his money. Georgia, in control of their home life, gives herself fully to her husband and his love.

Earlier in her quest, Catherine has returned with a friend to a lake she remembers from childhood, but is upset that the lake does not look the same. Her friend Samuel says, "But that's the way memory works . . . We supply the picture demanded by our imagination. And slowly, over time, it becomes what was."[27] This explanation disturbs Catherine. She remembers seeing a world below the lake, buildings submerged when the lake was dammed. If it was no more than her imagination, then is her grandparent's forgiveness no more than an illusion? She is relieved when Samuel writes that he has found her lake and it exists just as she had remembered it with a world below the water. It confirms for her that the world below her grandparent's relationship is an act of forgiveness that over the course of their lives allows them to reorder their relationship.

In reading this novel, the reader's imagination is expanded to see the possibility and complexity of forgiveness. The ambiguity of John's motives for sending Georgia to the sanitarium blurs the lines between victim and offender. Is Georgia the victim of John's abusive male power? Georgia sees herself as the victim of John's trickery. While John's motive as Georgia's physician was to insure her medical recovery, his personal motive was to increase his own control over her. This mixing of motives abuses the authority he had over her as doctor and male friend. Even though Georgia agreed to her treatment, she was the victim of manipulation. The subsequent affair with another patient and the resulting decision to help his family with burial expenses can be seen as the results of John's deception. John's confession to Catherine that he regretted the way he tried to control Georgia's life confirms his own culpability.

Other characters in the novel question this interpretation. Georgia's sister assumes that by referring to herself as "damaged goods" Georgia tricked John into marrying her under false pretenses. She labels the secretive appropriation of household funds as embezzlement and further proof of Georgia's manipulative behavior. While fully realizing the limited options for women in her grandmother's day and the damaging effects of her grandfather's behavior, Catherine does not see her grandmother as a mere victim. Catherine characterizes the use of money as an act of robbery and her grandfather as a victim of his wife's betrayal.

Miller invites the reader into the complexity of this relationship. Like Catherine, the reader is able to see both the sequence of events that abused trust and the decisions of both persons to use forms of control over the other. By describing the variety of interpretations that develop over the span of three generations, Miller is able to show how John's use of male authority led to abusive actions and Georgia's use of feminine deception abused John's trust. This breakdown of the categories of victim and offender show the full humanity of both persons without ignoring the different forms and degrees of power that are available to each of them. The result is that the reader can weep with Catherine for the pain that both suffered.

The beauty of this work is that it describes how the use of socially accepted forms of masculine and feminine control can lead to abuse. Feminist criticism has raised awareness about the misuse of traditional forms of masculine power, but it often fails to criticize traditional forms of feminine power. Gebara suggests that feminist theology needs to recognize the evil done by women as well as criticize the evil done to women. When culture subscribes women to the household realm their acts of violence can take the form of domestic intrigues, plots, and lies.[28] A truthful analysis needs to recognize these acts as abusive while at the same time exposing the damaging effects of cultural expectations that limit women's roles. Helping to see the complexity of the picture can help women and men accept accountability and render appropriate blame.

What this means is that John can see the power imbalance that is behind Georgia's actions. Giving Georgia money both acknowledges the power he has over the family finances and seeks to increase her financial freedom. By so doing, he eliminates the need for her to deceive him in the future. Catherine speculates that her grandfather's actions also pay restitution for admitting Georgia to the sanitarium. Thus he is able both to be accountable for his own actions and recognize his own victimization.

But for Georgia repentance and accountability are more difficult. John's act of restitution merely begins the process. Georgia makes peace with her life and begins a new role as mother. A few years later they move to a new town. But Georgia does not forget the events of her early marriage. Catherine feels a subtext of anger under the forgiving peace of her grandparent's marriage. Georgia does not confess repentance for her appropriation of household funds or ever tell Catherine the reason for taking them. She does tell Catherine she resents being sent to the sanitarium. As a teenager Catherine witnessed Georgia snap at John for pressuring Catherine to spend the summer in France. Catherine is shocked at the level of anger in her grandmother's voice. A few days later, Georgia confesses to Catherine that the sanitarium did open her to new options and change her in a positive way. By comparing her decision to go to the sanitarium with Catherine's decision to go to France, Georgia is finally able to accept accountability for the events that shaped her life.

Forgiveness is not a linear process, but rather moves in a spiral fashion between persons. Sometimes it takes a reliving of events through a third party to gain a larger perspective on the story of one's own life. In her study on women's experiences of evil and salvation, Gebara notes that we need to look for "moments of resurrection in daily life."[29] Miller does not isolate one event as the moment of forgiveness, but shows a series of moments in which John and Georgia live together through resentment and repentance to grow in their understanding of the other's actions and to accept accountability for their own.

The most significant factor in this process of forgiveness is the ability to remember the past in a positive way. As the title to Miller's novel suggests, there is a "world below" forgiveness. Numerous scholars have suggested the crucial role of memory in the process of forgiveness. Volf calls it the ability to recast the past in a non-tragic future. Kristeva defines forgiveness as finding meaning beyond non-meaning. In Georgia's ability to see how the sanitarium opened her to the future, Miller shows the reader this process of recasting the past into a meaningful future. This interpretation helps Georgia see her affair, her marriage, and even her illness as more than damaging events. They are the opening scenes of the larger narrative of her good and lasting relationship with John.

Feminists have been critical of the counsel to forgive and forget because it encourages women to remain victimized by abuse. But the lesson to be learned from this novel is that refusing to let go can also trap a person in a cycle of self-abuse. It is necessary to recast the memory of past hurt in order to forgive and it is appropriate to do so in relationships that work to restore the balance of power and control. John's awareness of his accountability certainly makes this a relationship worth saving. But all his efforts to make amends cannot erase Georgia's feeling that she is "damaged goods." Only when Georgia herself is ready to let go of this self-image can she forgive.

What differentiates this novel from Miller's earlier works is the ability to remember the past in a way that forgets past hurt. As was mentioned earlier in this article Miller has been writing about unforgiving relationships for over a decade. When she writes about relationships between abusive parents and their children the reader is relieved that Miller does not create a happy ending that is based on a cheap and false sense of forgiveness. In the instance of the adult son who forgives his mother after her death, the reader is satisfied that the son sees the truth of his mother's abusive behavior and has learned to move positively beyond it into the future. But in other instances, such as the parent who is falsely accused of child abuse or the couples who cannot overcome acts of betrayal by their spouses, the reader longs for a vision of reconciliation. It is this ability of Georgia and John to see the past truly and yet move forward to a healthy relationship that makes for the happiest of endings. Readers familiar with all of Miller's novels will recognize that the lesson is not that forgiveness is always possible or desired but that a wholesale rejection of forgiveness is as unrealistic as the wholesale mandate to forgive and forget.

By narrating the story through Catherine's loving eyes, rather than Georgia's damaged perspective, Miller gives the reader a point of view that transcends Georgia's own understanding. Catherine is able to compare her own recollections to Georgia's diaries and household ledgers. Miller skillfully uses past record and present memory to broaden the reader's perspective. This allows Miller to develop what she describes as a "godlike" perspective[30] that understands things about Georgia that she does not see in herself.

The idea of a "godlike" perspective is suggestive of the religious dimension of memory. Catherine's friend is skeptical of memory because it distorts the historical record, but Catherine holds to the hope that memory is more than wishful imagination. She knows that there is something more to her grandparent's relationship, and it is something that she failed to have in her own marriages. What she discovers is that both grandparents are able to transcend their own perspectives at crucial points in their relationship. By opening the bank account John is able to transcend his need for control, and by coming to terms with her treatment Georgia is able to transcend her hurt.

Such moments are acts of grace, noble gestures that are rare in life, but realistic and possible. The greatest benefit of this story is that it describes quiet and common nobility that enables forgiveness. Miller challenges her readers to think beyond the kind of religious interpretation that hopes for supernatural acts of God. Grace is realized in the possibility of utilizing our God-given ability to remember. Forgiveness requires a kind of transcendence that develops from our natural abilities, helps us see beyond our ability, and enables us to be more than victims, more than offenders, more than well-adjusted survivors. Forgiveness is the possibility of living fully in the image of God.

A theology of forgiveness must likewise realize the complexity of forgiveness in a way that discerns when and where forgiveness is desirable, and in such instances sees beyond the labels of victim and offender all the while realizing the nuances of accountability, celebrating the grace of memory, and enabling persons to grasp the nobility of forgiveness. It is this natural nobility rather than the heroic nobility of self-sacrificial love that best embodies forgiveness. Our thanks to Sue Miller for creating the space that allows us to imagine the practice of forgiveness.

NOTES

1. Sue Miller, *The World Below* (New York: Alfred Knopf, 2001), 266. Other novels by Miller include *The Good Mother* (New York: Harper and Row, 1986); *Family Pictures* (San Francisco: Harper and Row, 1990); *For Love* (San Francisco: Harper and Row, 1993); *The Distinguished Guest* (New York: Harper Collins, 1995); and *While I Was Gone* (New York: Ballantine Books, 1999).

2. Millicent Feske, "Mistaking Death for Life: Thelma and Louise and Tashi and the Christian Construction of Redemption," *Journal of Religion & Abuse* 1:1 (1999): 30. Feske's focus is on redemption rather than forgiveness, but her insights are germane to this topic. Her study turns to the problematic vision of redemption in the movie *Thelma and Louise* and the novel *Possessing the Secret of Joy*. She calls for studying narratives that provide positive examples of salvation. The study of Miller's novel as a positive example of forgiveness is an answer to her call.

3. L. Gregory Jones, *Embodying Forgiveness: A Theological Analysis* (Grand Rapids: Eerdmans Publishing Company, 1995).

4. Miroslav Volf, *Exclusion and Embrace: A Theological Exploration of Identity, Otherness, and Reconciliation* (Nashville: Abingdon Press, 1996), 26, 29,105. This book received the 2001 Grawemeyer award for the best book in theology.

5. Ivone Gebara, *Out of the Depths: Women's Experience of Evil and Salvation* (Minneapolis: Fortress Press, 2002), 71. There are a whole host of critiques of the Christian theory of forgiveness by feminist theologians. One of the earliest is Marie Fortune, *Keeping the Faith: Questions and Answers for the Abused Woman* (San Francisco: Harper and Row, 1987), 46-51. For a few recent articles see Susan Hylen, "Forgiveness and Life in Community," *Interpretation* 54:2 (April 2000): 146-157; and Joretta Marshall, "Forgiving Churches: Avenues of Hope for Rural Communities," *Word and World* 20:2 (Spring 2000): 188-192.

6. This critique is not a dismissal of the importance of these theological studies. Both have insight about forgiveness that will be used in the analysis of Miller's novel. Volf's definition of memory as that which recasts the past into a non-tragic future is an insightful contribution to the role of memory in the work of forgiveness. Volf, 133. Likewise, Jones' use of narratives in his study on forgiveness set a precedent for this review of Miller's novel.

7. Aurel Kolnar in Hylen, 149.

8. Ruth Kluger, "Forgiving and Remembering," *PMLA* 117:2 (March 2002): 313.

9. Martha Minnow, *Between Vengeance and Forgiveness: Facing History after Genocide and Mass Violence* (Boston: Beacon Press, 1998), 21.

10. Cary Nelson, "Forgiveness and the Social Psyche," *PMLA* 117:2 (March 2002): 318.

11. The International Forgiveness Institute is based at the University of Wisconsin, Madison, and directed by Robert Enrich, professor of educational psychology. It began with research in 1985 and the Institute was established in 1994. For information see http://www.forgiveness-institute.org.

12. Virginia Holeman and Rita Myers, "Effects of Forgiveness of Perpetrators on Marital Adjustment for Survivors of Sexual Abuse," *Family Journal* 5:4 (October 1997): 182-189. Also see Suzanne Freedman, "Forgiveness as an Intervention Goal with Incest Survivors," *Journal of Consulting and Clinical Psychology* 64 (October 1996): 883-992. The Freedman study of incest survivors has similar conclusions.

13. See Julia Kristeva, "Forgiveness: An Interview," *PMLA* 117:2 (March 2002): 281-282. Another important French study is Paul Ricoeur, *La mémoire, l'historie, l'oubli* (Paris: Seuil, 2000).

14. Wayne Booth, *The Company We Keep: An Ethics of Fiction* (Berkeley: UC Press, 1988), 260, 287. Booth quotes Martha Nussbaum for observing that narratives have the benefit of displaying the complexity of moral choice in a way that cannot be done in the universalizing language of philosophy. See Booth, 43-44. Readers familiar with narrative theology will note that there are questions about the truth status of narra-

tives, especially works of fiction, for theological reflection. For a critical review see Keith Yandell, ed., *Faith and Narrative* (Oxford: Oxford Press, 2001). I agree with Booth that the books we read do shape our imaginations and lead us to truth.

15. Booth, 360.

16. William Pritchard, review of *While I Was Gone*, by Sue Miller, *Commonweal* 126:21 (December 3 1999): 23.

17. Ray Parini, review of *The Good Mother*, by Sue Miller, *New York Times Book Review* 148: 51440 (February 21 1999): 10-11.

18. Elfreida Abbe, "Diving Deep," *Writer* 115:4 (April 2002): 31.

19. Miller, *Family Pictures*, 369.

20. Miller, *For Love*, 234.

21. Miller, *The World Below*, 205. This event is filled with ambiguity. There was no definitive cure for tuberculosis in the early 20th century, but bed rest seemed to give those who were capable of fighting the infection a better chance of recovery. John knew that Georgia was likely not to die from the disease, but her responsibilities as her father's housekeeper could weaken her. Georgia's complaint is that he did not tell her the whole truth or allow her to make the decision about treatment. She is left wondering if she has married a manipulative man rather than the forgiving person she had imagined him to be. The reader is left pondering John's motives and wondering if betrayal of trust, even if one is well intentioned, can be forgiven.

22. Miller, *The World Below*, 265.

23. Miller, *The World Below*, 266.

24. Miller, *The World Below*, 123.

25. Miller, *The World Below*, 124.

26. Jeff Zeleski, review of *The World Below*, by Sue Miller, *Publisher's Weekly* 248:29 (July 16 2001): 166.

27. Miller, *The World Below*, 211. Samuel is a historian who exemplifies the modern skepticism that all past memories are works of fiction.

28. Gebara, 97.

29. This phrase comes from Gebara, 138.

30. Abbe, 30.

REFERENCES

Abbe, Elfreida. "Diving Deep." *Writer* 115:4 (April 2002): 26-31.

Booth, Wayne. *The Company We Keep: An Ethics of Fiction*. Berkeley: UC Press, 1988.

Feske, Millicent. "Mistaking Death for Life: Thelma and Louise and Tashi and the Christian Construction of Redemption." *Journal of Religion & Abuse* 1:1 (1999): 15-35.

Fortune, Marie. *Keeping the Faith: Questions and Answers for the Abused Woman*. San Francisco: Harper and Row, 1987.

Freedman, Suzanne. "Forgiveness as an Intervention Goal with Incest Survivors." *Journal of Consulting and Clinical Psychology* 64 (October 1996): 883-992.

Gebara, Ivone. *Out of the Depths: Women's Experience of Evil and Salvation*. Minneapolis: Fortress Press, 2002.

Holeman, Virginia and Rita Myers. "Effects of Forgiveness of Perpetrators on Marital Adjustment for Survivors of Sexual Abuse." *Family Journal* 5:4 (October 1997): 182-189.

Hylen, Susan. "Forgiveness and Life in Community." *Interpretation* 54:2 (April 2000): 146-157. The International Forgiveness Institute. http://www.forgiveness-institute.org.

Jones, L. Gregory. *Embodying Forgiveness: A Theological Analysis.* Grand Rapids: Eerdmans Publishing Company, 1995.

Kluger, Ruth. "Forgiving and Remembering." *PMLA* 117:2 (March 2002): 311-313.

Kristeva, Julia. "Forgiveness: An Interview." *PMLA* 117:2 (March 2002): 278-287.

Marshall, Joretta. "Forgiving Churches: Avenues of Hope for Rural Communities." *Word and World* 20:2 (Spring 2000): 188-192.

Miller, Sue. *The Distinguished Guest.* New York: Harper Collins, 1995.

_____. *Family Pictures.* San Francisco: Harper and Row, 1990.

_____. *For Love.* San Francisco: Harper and Row, 1993.

_____. *The Good Mother.* New York: Harper and Row, 1986.

_____. *While I Was Gone.* New York: Ballantine Books, 1999.

_____. *The World Below.* New York: Alfred Knopf, 2001.

Minnow, Martha. *Between Vengeance and Forgiveness: Facing History after Genocide and Mass Violence.* Boston: Beacon Press, 1998.

Nelson, Cary. "Forgiveness and the Social Psyche." *PMLA* 117:2 (March 2002): 317-319.

Parini, Jay. Review of *The Good Mother,* by Sue Miller. *New York Times Book Review* 148:51440 (February 21, 1999): 10-11.

Pritchard, William. Review of *While I Was Gone,* by Sue Miller. *Commonweal* 126:21 (December 3 1999): 22-24.

Ricoeur, Paul. La mémorie, l'historie, l'oubli. Paris: Seuil, 2000.

Volf, Miroslav. *Exclusion and Embrace: A Theological Exploration of Identity, Otherness, and Reconciliation.* Nashville: Abingdon Press, 1996.

Yandell, Keith. Ed. *Faith and Narrative.* Oxford: Oxford Press, 2001.

Zeleski, Jeff. Review of *The World Below,* by Sue Miller. *Publisher's Weekly* 248:29 (July 16 2001): 166.

Index

Abuse, as life disruption, 114,119
Accountability, 65
Ambivalence, 110
Amnesty, vs. forgiveness, 111-112, 119
Anger, 102-103
Apartheid, 65-66,111-112,119
Atonement, 117-118
Avoidance, in clergy sexual abuse, 58-59

Behavioral change, repentance and, 121-124
Booth, Wayne, 138

Center for Epidemiologic Studies Depression Scale, 35,37
Center for the Prevention of Sexual and Domestic Violence, 63-64
Christian tradition, 2
   as avoidance strategy, 58-59
   deconstruction and, 58-59
   ethical issues and, 51-70
   justice and clergy abuse, 71-88
   mental health and, 31-33,41-43, 45-47
   misconceptions about forgiveness, 54-57
   moral agency and, 57-58
   patriarchal aspects, 60-61
   power issues in abuse, 64-66, 118-120
   proactive mandate, 54

reconstruction and, 59-68
Russell's theological spiral, 57
unforgiveness and, 54-55
Clergy sexual abuse, 71-88
   behavioral change, 78-79
   of children, 80-85
   by Christian clergy, 52-54
   collective *vs.* personal absolution, 79
   forgiveness as avoidance, 58-59
   ordination as covenant, 76
   perpetrator's claiming forgiveness, 74-75
   power issues, 64-66,118-120
   repentance and, 79
   restitution as required, 77-80
   therapy as restitution, 75-76
Cognitive rehearsal, 100
Collusion, 121. *See also* Religious complicity
Community aspects, Samoan model, 66-68
Confession, 120. *See also* Truthtelling
Contrition, 65

Day of Atonement. *See* Yom Kippur
Decision phase of forgiveness, 100-101
Deepening phase of forgiveness, 101-102
Defense mechanisms, 98-100
Demographics, midwestern mental health study, 30-40,35
Depression, 43
Dispositional forgiveness, 44-45
(The) Distinguished Guest (Miller), 139